A LAYMAN LOOKS AT THE LOVE OF GOD

Devotional Study of 1 Corinthians 13

W. PHILLIP KELLER

BETHANY HOUSE PUBLISHERS

MINNEAPOLIS, MINNESOTA 55438

A Division of Bethany Fellowship, Inc.

*Proceeds from the sale of this book go to
Bethany Fellowship for missionary training.*

Scripture verses are taken from the King James Version of the Bible
unless otherwise noted.

Published by Bethany House Publishers
A Division of Bethany Fellowship, Inc.
6820 Auto Club Road, Minneapolis, Minnesota 55438

Printed in the United States of America

Library of Congress Cataloging in Publication Data

Keller, W. Phillip (Weldon Phillip), 1920-
    A layman looks at the love of God.

    1. God—Love.   2. Bible. N.T. Corinthians, 1st XIII
—Criticism, interpretation, etc. I. Title.
BT140.K45   1984 $231^1.6$ 84-16857

ISBN 0-87123-618-4

To
"CHERI"—
My happy companion
who reflects
the love of God.

A Word of Thanks

A note of appreciation is due to Mr. Dave Thomas of Montecito, California, who provided me with tapes of the talks I gave to the Montecito Covenant Church on the topic of The Love of God.

Again I am genuinely grateful to "Cheri," my wife Ursula, for the time and care she devoted to typing the manuscript.

Also a great debt of love is owed to those dear people across the continent, who, in the early hours of the morning, pray for me as I write. Their loyal faithfulness is a precious honour.

Most important is the distinct direction and guidance given in this book by Christ Himself. In a very personal way His Love has been manifested to me in this work. *What an honour!*

Table of Contents

1

And yet I show you a more excellent way.

Though I speak with the tongues of men and of angels, but have not love, I have become as sounding brass or a clanging cymbal.

And though I have the gift of prophecy, and understand all mysteries and all knowledge, and though I have all faith, so that I could remove mountains, but have not love, I am nothing.

And though I bestow all my goods to feed the poor, and though I give my body to be burned, but have not love, it profits me nothing.

Love suffers long and is kind; love does not envy; love does not parade itself, is not puffed up; does not behave rudely, does not seek its own, is not provoked, thinks no evil; does not rejoice in iniquity, but rejoices in the truth; bears all things, believes all things, hopes all things, endures all things.

Love never fails. But whether there are prophecies, they will fail; whether there is knowledge, it will vanish away.

For we know in part and we prophesy in part.

But when that which is perfect has come, then that which is in part will be done away.

When I was a child, I spoke as a child, I understood as a child, I thought as a child; but when I became a man, I put away childish things.

For now we see in a mirror, dimly, but then face to face. Now I know in part, but then I shall know just as I also am known.

And now abide faith, hope, love, these three; but the greatest of these is love.

PURSUE LOVE. . . .

1 Corinthians 12:31–14:1, NKJV

THE CHARACTER OF CHRIST

For roughly fifteen years various earnest people, eager to know God, have asked me to write a book on "The Character of Christ." Some of these thirsty, seeking ones have been ordinary lay people like myself. Others are scholars, pastors and teachers.

This book is my third serious attempt to respond to that compelling inner cry of the human spirit, "Oh, that I might know God, Whom to know is life eternal" (see John 17:3). For when all else is said and done, a man's greatest and highest goal in life is to enjoy intimate communion with Christ.

The keen companionship which can be developed and cultivated between Christ, who is God very God, and a humble human being is based upon a clear understanding of His character. Not until we come to perceive clearly with our spirits the true nature of Christ and what a sublime person He is do we ever actually draw near to Him or allow Him to draw near to us.

The first book I wrote to portray the true character

of Christ was *A Shepherd Looks at Psalm 23,* based on the Spirit's revelation in the Old Testament of Christ as our Good Shepherd. The second earnest endeavour to convey this theme to the reader was the book *Rabboni—Which Is to Say, Master,* based on the Gospel records given to us in the New Testament. It is perhaps by far the most important book I have ever written. It reveals Christ as God, very God, in human garb.

This book is based largely on the teaching of God's gracious Spirit given to us in the New Testament Epistles, with special emphasis upon the statements made so emphatically in the "Love Chapter," 1 Corinthians 13. Before we go further, we must clarify a few fundamental truths.

The first basic concept is that *the character of Christ* is essentially *the life of God*—or, to use an ancient term, *the very nature of God.* If we wish to know God as He really is, then we must perceive Him as portrayed in the person of Christ. "Christ is the visible expression of the invisible God" (Col. 1:15, Phillips).

The second foundation truth is that *the life of God* revealed to us in *the character of Christ* is in essence *the love of God*, "for God is love" (1 John 4:8). Or to put all of this in the most fundamental terms, we can understand something of the intrinsic character of Christ as we comprehend more clearly the love of God.

The third point to grasp with our spiritual understanding is that the phrase *love of God* does not refer to our love for God but rather *His love for us*, that quality of His own divine life which emanates from

Him to us in a wondrous outpouring. There flows eternally to the family of men a stream of self-giving from God. It finds expression in a thousand generous gestures all intended for our good. "Every good gift and every perfect gift is from above, and cometh down from the Father of lights, with whom is no variableness, neither shadow of turning" (James 1:17).

The fourth basic truth is that this generous, gracious self-giving of God to us in Christ by His Spirit becomes for the Christian the greatest and most important reality in all of life. In point of fact, the realization that *God is with me . . . Christ is in me . . . His Spirit occupies my spirit* becomes the compelling relationship, the divine impetus, that causes my character to change and transforms me into someone of His own likeness. "For it is God which worketh in you both to will and to do of his good pleasure" (Phil. 2:13).

The fifth foundation truth to grasp is that not only does God's Spirit reveal to us the fact that He resides in us, but also that *it is possible for us to live in Christ.* A Christian comes to the comprehension in very practical terms that it is "in him [God] we live, and move, and have our being. . ." (Acts 17:28). The child of God recognizes that his entire life is bound up in the enfolding goodness of God, expressed to him in the love of God.

The sixth basic concept is that as one comes to commune with Christ in this intense interrelationship, *His presence becomes increasingly more precious.* To know Him, enjoy Him, obey Him, serve Him and love Him becomes the ultimate fulfillment in life. Paul, in his letter to the Philippians, put it this way: "I count all things but loss for the excellency of the knowledge of Christ Jesus my Lord . . ." (Phil. 3:8).

The seventh and last truth is that for our life in Christ to prosper and His life in us to flourish, *our attention must be focused upon Him.* He simply *must* occupy the prior position in all our interests. Time, thought, prayer and meditation in quiet interludes with Him are imperative. Then this scripture will become a reality in our lives: "If anyone is in Christ, he is a new creation; old things have passed away; behold, all things have become new" (2 Cor. 5:17, NKJV).

This total transformation of our lives is an ongoing process. This means having the very character of Christ transmitted and transferred to us. It is to actually know and experience the incoming of the life of God into our tiny, human lives. It is to sense and know the very love of God shed abroad in our spirits by His Spirit (Rom. 5:5).

There is no doubt whatsoever that ultimately this is the most intense inner desire of anyone who earnestly longs to know God. Therefore, it is without apology that as a lay person I undertake to share with the reader some of those insights which God's gracious Spirit has given to me on this magnificent subject.

I am fully aware that perhaps more sermons in this century have been given on "The Love of God" than any other theme. More books have been written about it than any other spiritual subject. More emphasis has been given to it than probably any other aspect of Christian life within the church.

Yet, despite this deluge of material, both oral and written, it is my simple prayer that Our Father will see fit to honour this little book with His smile of approval. My desire is that through it the reader will come to a clearer comprehension of Christ's character, and that in reading these pages, God's Spirit will impart the very life and love of God to the reader.

For this to take place there is a sense in which a person must literally plunge into and drink deeply from the stream of life that flows to us from God Himself. This is not mere figurative language. If we are to know Christ and experience His love in daily reality, we cannot stand at a distance and simply discuss it doctrinally. We must come to Him and drink of His divine life, partake of His very nature.

This book, written in simple layman's language, using word pictures and the most practical terms possible, endeavours to help the reader to know the love of God. The "knowing" of which I speak is both in the wondrous expression of the life of Jesus Our Lord and in His winsome operation within our own souls and spirits. It is both an outward, objective observation and a profound, personal, inner, subjective experience. It is both the love of God as revealed in His own conduct and character and the very life of God worked out through our lives in this weary, sin-stained world.

To know this love of God is to be totally immersed in the stream of life which flows to us from Him. In human society we speak freely of being in "the stream of life," the area or discipline in which we choose to involve ourselves. It may be in business or science or music or the arts or the humanities or travel or athletics. To plunge fully into the interest or vocation of our own choosing and to drink deeply of all it has to offer is part and parcel of succeeding in any given arena of life.

Likewise for the Christian, if we are to find complete satisfaction in Christ, there is no other way than to submerge ourselves in the stream of His life. We need to come to Him and drink deeply of His love. We must find our refreshment, our constant reinvigoration, in His consistent character. Here lies the secret to quiet serenity, confident strength and sure stability amid all the changing circumstances which face a Christian in today's world.

In Psalm 42 we are given a beautiful word picture of a deer in distress. It is being pursued by the hunters and their hounds in the hills. For safety and survival it rushes down the slopes and into the stream.

There in the cooling, refreshing current that flows from the snow-mantled mountains its thirst is slaked; its safety is assured; its survival is guaranteed. This dramatic poem written under the inspiration of God's Spirit portrays precisely the elements inherent in the picture of a man or woman plunging fully into the refreshing, protecting fullness of God's life and love, finding total salvation amid life's strains and stresses.

It is a vivid metaphor that will be developed in much greater detail in a later chapter. It is the basic background against which this devotional study of 1 Corinthians 13 has been written. So I invite the reader to carefully and prayerfully peruse the pages which follow. Please do not hold yourself aloof, examining what has been written with only academic and objective interest. Instead, allow God's Spirit to so immerse you in Christ's love that His very life shall become your life, His character your character.

This is what it means to come to Christ, to drink of Him, to know Him, to relish Him.

As I pen these lines I am vividly reminded of an in-
cident that took place during my early teens, roughly
fifty years ago. My dad and mother were literally
laying down their lives to try and establish a strong
group of Christian believers in the bush country of
Kenya. But after working tirelessly for sixteen years
in that difficult territory, they decided a special,
deeper work of God was needed. Only God's Spirit
and God's Word could inspire and lead men and
women to immerse themselves in the very life of
Christ.

With this goal in mind, a conference was held.
Every one of the Christian leaders, pastors, teachers
and elders was obliged to attend. In preparation for
the week's conference, each one was to read and
meditate on 1 Corinthians 13. The entire chapter was
to be prayed over carefully every day for a full month!
It was also to be completely memorized and repeated
whenever the Holy Spirit brought it to their attention.
The leaders were to submerge themselves in these
scriptures.

When they came to the conference, held in a very
simple, sheet-iron chapel on the crest of a high hill,
it was to study and examine and understand what
God's Spirit was conveying to the church in this profound passage. For seven days and seven nights that
group of African Christians dwelt in the truths of this
so-called *Love Chapter*. In doing so, they came to
Christ; they drank deeply of His life; they were
satisfied; their thirst was slaked. And they went away
revitalized.

The results of that event were absolutely dramatic.
In the lives of the leaders there came an acute and

unique awareness of Christ within. It began to change the whole character of the African church. There was a tremendous new thrust in the work of God's Spirit among those who longed to know God. A great sense of earnestness and devotion to Christ developed. Perhaps most profound for me as a lad was to see the beginning of an enormous change in my dad's character. Where before he had been rather rough and tough, there began to steal over his life a winsome, mellow tenderness. He became one dearly beloved. He was approachable, understanding and patient in ways never known before.

This was the unique impact of the character of Christ upon his character. In awe and gratitude I saw in living terms what the love of God could do. My most earnest prayer is that the pages which follow may be used of God in the same way for you.

2

*"Yet I show you
a more excellent
way. Though I
speak with the
tongues of men
and of angels,
but have not love,
I have become as
sounding brass
or a clanging
cymbal."*

(1 Cor. 12:31; 13:1, NKJV)

THE MORE EXCELLENT WAY

God Himself has given us a remarkable revelation of His own love in Scripture. It comes with startling significance in the very center of the Spirit's most detailed discourse on God's special "gifts" to the church. It stands there with towering grandeur as a call to all Christians: *the more excellent way in which the church can know Christ and live for Him in this world is through His love and by His life.*

This thirteenth chapter of the first letter to the carnal church at Corinth is a compelling description of Christ's character. Here is the divine declaration of Christian attitude and behavior, the way in which Christ Himself calls us to conduct ourselves as His followers—His people, His Bride. It is the great central theme around which all other considerations in the church are of secondary consequence and peripheral importance.

This dazzling revelation of Christ's divine love, like a diamond, outshines with burning brilliance all the other precious gems of God's gifts. With enormous power and value it transcends all other unique capacities given to the church for service. It is Christ Himself—His love—His life that is "the more excellent way."

The sensual, self-serving Corinthians were challenged with this message. And the Spirit of God speaks the same heart-stirring word to the sensual, pleasure-seeking church of the Twentieth Century.

Today's church worldwide, as in the days of Paul, has become unduly preoccupied with the spectacular. It pursues power and growth and social acceptance without purity. It is eager for miracles and manifestations, often with very wrong motives. It revels in the sensational, often being diverted into that which is grossly sensual, all in the name of "spiritual gifts."

It is the age-old tendency, present in Corinth as well, to become more attracted to the "gifts" than to The Giver of those gifts . . . of being busy rather than being bountiful . . . of being "on the go" rather than being godly.

The consequence for the church has been to forget that it is The Lord Jesus Christ who is its Head. He it is who stands supreme amongst us, yet who so often has become almost a stranger to us.

Writing on this theme, David Wilkerson makes this solemn, yet valid observation: "I say to you, it is possible to gather Spirit-filled people in one place, praising and lifting up their hands—and still have Christ walking among them as a stranger. . . . We make Christ a stranger—by giving the Holy Spirit preeminence over Him."

It is for this very reason that God's Gracious Spirit speaks emphatically to this point, declaring unequivocally at the end of 1 Corinthians 12: *"Yet I show you a more excellent way."* He calls us back to the love of God, exemplified for us in the character of the living Christ.

Using the persuasive power of contrast, He then proceeds to compare the gifts bestowed with the life of The Giver. He holds up to full view our folly in being so taken up with our gifts that the very life of God is lacking in our activities and conduct.

Sensational, blood-stirring, nerve-tingling services filled with "faith," "prophecies," "miracles" and "tongues" all amount to nothing . . . nothing . . . *nothing* without God's love.

This is a most serious indictment! It should pull us up short. It shatters and pulverizes our pride in performance!

This solemn call to examine our own characters in the intense light of the love of God is almost as solemn as Our Lord's cataclysmic statement in Matthew 7:21-23: "Not everyone that saith unto me, Lord, Lord, shall enter into the kingdom of heaven. Many will say to me in that day, Lord, Lord, have we not prophesied in thy name? and in thy name have cast out devils? and in thy name done many wonderful works? And then will I profess unto them, I never knew you: depart from me, ye that work iniquity."

We begin with a basic understanding of what God's Spirit means when He speaks of God's love.

As many readers no doubt have heard explained, there are three types of love. Each of them has its origin with God. It is He who devised and designed these expressions for the benefit of mankind. Yet it must be understood that of these three, only one (the

third point discussed in the following list) is referred
to in the thirteenth chapter of 1 Corinthians.

1. There is filial love, so-called "family" love, the
affection that flows freely throughout the family of
man. It is sometimes called the "milk of human kindness." We see it reflected and displayed in the intimate
bonds of love between parents and children, brothers
and sisters, friends in sports, business partners, or
even soldiers in war.

It is that element of loyalty, devotion and concern
which enables one human being to lay down his life
for another who is a friend or family member. Jesus
Christ referred to this as the greatest love there is in
the human family (John 15:13).

This fraternal love is found even amongst pagan
people.

2. Then there is erotic or so-called sexual love.
This is the profound and powerful attraction between
people of opposite sexes. It, too, was designed and
arranged by God for the preservation and intimacy
of the family of man. It was intended for the perpetu-
ation of the race.

This kind of love is to be found amongst all people all
over the earth. In its proper role as the instigator and
protector of the family, it is a beautiful bond of human
behavior. Within the framework of a home and in the
cherished intimacy between true life mates it is beautiful
beyond words to describe.

Unhappily, it has been eternally prostituted and perverted by the sordid minds of unregenerate men and
women. Consequently, many modern references to this
sort of love tend to be more beastly than beautiful.

3. Lastly there is the profound love of God referred to

so often in the New Testament. As pointed out in the previous chapter, this love of God does not denote our human "love for God," as we sometimes state so glibly, "for love of God and country." Rather, this love of God is uniquely and amazingly *His love toward us.* It is His care and concern and affection for us even while we were still His enemies. (Please take a moment here to read and meditate on Rom. 5:5-11.)

Human beings with filial love lay down their lives for their friends and family.

But Our Father in Heaven, the source of divine love, lays down His life for His *enemies*, we who were alienated from Him. In Christ we see this love poured out for men who hate Him and vilify Him, who are determined to destroy Him. Despite their animosity, He in love comes to seek and to save.

This *agape* love, as it is called in the original Greek, is vested only in God. It comes only from Him. It is epitomized in the very character of Christ. It can only be imparted to us by His Own Spirit.

This love of God is essentially His utter selflessness as opposed to our self-centeredness. It is His self-giving as opposed to our self-getting. It is His generous self-sharing as opposed to our self-gratification. It is His self-sacrifice as opposed to our self-indulgence.

In His generous, gracious manner, Christ longs to convey this quality of His own life and character to us. But far too often we are so preoccupied with our own personal pursuits and selfish pride that He is given very little opportunity to bestow His own life on us. There is little stillness or solitude in which His Spirit can shed abroad such love within our spirits.

We of the busy, boisterous and clamorous Twentieth Century would much rather get on with the glitter and excitement of our own interests and special gifts. After all, who is interested in laying down their lives when all around us people are shouting, even from the pulpit, that we should be "living it up," "living life to the full"?

This is the very first contrast that God's Spirit draws for us in the almost formidable language of the opening verse of this wonderful chapter: "Though I speak with the tongues of men and of angels, but have not love, I have become as sounding brass or a clanging cymbal" (1 Cor. 13:1, NKJV).

What a commentary on contemporary society, both inside and outside the church! At no time in human history has there been so much emphasis on communication—on human and celestial "tongues," breaching the barriers of known and unknown language. The power and impact of the media to bear a message, no matter how "brassy," is unsurpassed in history.

People with all sorts of destructive propaganda, the most blatant deception, have their followers. Inspiring leaders can capture the attention of the masses by their eloquence and ·magnetism alone.

Both within the family of God and outside, multitudes are lured into believing lies by the smooth eloquence and clever use of the tongue. People are led to think they are receiving truth when in fact it is often false teaching.

It is significant that the first aspect of the Christian life to be addressed by God's Spirit in this passage is the use of language without love. It is the question of our conversation without the accompanying quality of Christ's genuine, self-giving courtesy. It is the manipulation of others with words which carry no sincerity. It is the absence of integrity in our communication with others. Christ states emphatically: "Either make the tree good, and his fruit good; or else make the tree corrupt: for the tree is known by his fruit. O generation of vipers, how can ye, being evil, speak good things? for out of the abundance of the heart the mouth speaketh. A good man out of the good treasure of the heart bringeth forth good things: and an evil man out of the evil treasure bringeth forth evil things. But I say unto you, That every idle word that men shall speak, they shall give account thereof in the day of judgment. For by thy words thou shalt be justified, and by thy words thou shalt be condemned" (Matt. 12:33-37).

Few Christians today take these statements seriously. Much of their conversation is double-tongued, double-edged, with more than one meaning, a carry-over from our own corrupt society. It is alarming how often those who claim their special spiritual gifts from God as a sign of His infilling actually defame His name with their own duplicity. Both in their personal conversation and in their business transactions, this pernicious double-standard of speaking and acting brings shame to Christ.

Christ Himself used the metaphor of a fruit tree to make this fact clear to His generation. And through a vivid experience with a wild apple tree I, too, learned this important principle as a young man.

On the first ranch I owned, there was an ancient homestead. The early pioneers had planted an orchard. All the trees had ultimately perished before I had come on the scene. But near the rough, old rock foundation of the original frontier house I found a single, vigorous apple tree crowded in by dense brush and wild brambles.

The discovery that first year excited me, though the tree bore no fruit. So I got busy and cleared away all the encroaching undergrowth. In the winter I took hours to prune the tree with painstaking care. In the early spring it was sprayed against disease.

The magnificent-looking tree burst into a billowing cloud of exquisite pink and white blossoms, many of which set fruit. And as the summer progressed the whole tree leafed out into a magnificent display of green glory. Never had I seen such a majestic apple tree so laden with a promising crop of fruit.

As summer moved on into the golden autumn, I could hardly restrain myself from immediately gathering some of the apples. They formed into large heavy fruit that weighed down the branches in their abundance. What a sight! What a show!

At last the time came to sample the crop. To my utter chagrin and total dismay, the fruit was worthless! It had no flavour; it was unfit even to cook or preserve. We never were able to eat one of the apples! It was but a wild seedling!

All the work, the care, the pruning, the spraying was of no avail. All the size and strength of the tree, its beauty, its blossoms, its abundant crop was but a "show," a sham.

God's Spirit used that wild, untamed tree to teach me a cardinal Christian principle I have never forgotten: "It is by their fruits you shall know them."

It is not by our eloquent language, not by our capacity to communicate, not by our charm or charis-

ma, not by our special gifts of "tongues," whether
natural or supernatural, that we shall be known as
God's children. Rather it is by our conversation—
what we say and how we say it—when it conveys
the integrity of Christ's own character.

The mark of the person whose spirit is laden with
the fruit of the love of God is a wise tongue, a trained
tongue, a tempered tongue.

Such a person's conversation will have complete
credibility. He will speak in honesty, wisdom, and
with transparent sincerity.

Communication with others should be a benefit
and benediction. It should be used to build up the
weak and to encourage the strong. It will be courteous
and kind.

Our language must not be tainted by indecent
frivolity or worldly foolishness. It should convey healing humour, wholesome laughter and good cheer for
heavy hearts.

The tongue of a true child of God will speak often
of the goodness of God, Our Father, the presence of
Christ, and the sure guidance of God's Gracious Spirit
along life's tangled trails.

Any such "word fitly spoken is like apples of gold
in pitchers of silver" (Prov. 25:11).

3

"And though
I have the gift
of prophecy, and
understand all
mysteries and all
knowledge, and
though I have all
faith, so that I
could remove
mountains, but
have not love,
I am nothing."

(1 Cor. 13:2, NKJV)

PROPHECY, KNOWLEDGE AND FAITH, WITHOUT LOVE, ARE SIMPLY OF NO ACCOUNT

The next three great gifts of the Spirit with which God's love is compared are prophecy, spiritual knowledge, and faith. In the evaluation of most Christians, these three would stand supreme in the service of the church.

It would be helpful if we look at each of these in detail. We should understand their role in the modern setting of Twentieth-Century society. Most importantly, we must see the enormous prominence given to them by our contemporary church leaders.

Yet ever in the background there stands this solemn statement of God's Spirit of Truth: all prophecy, all knowledge, and all faith are of no value without love. This startles us. It should stir us to ask, "Why?" It should stab us wide awake as to what is of greatest worth in God's view. Perhaps our priorities and spiritual emphasis in the pulpit have become reversed and confused when compared with what Christ considers to be of primary importance.

Before doing this, however, it is essential that the reader should grasp the great difference between (a) the "gifts" of God's Spirit and (b) the "fruits" of God's Spirit. There is genuine confusion in many Christian circles over this matter; this is the reason they are especially contrasted here.

1. The fruits of God's Spirit—love, joy, peace, longsuffering, gentleness, goodness, faith, meekness, temperance (Gal. 5:22-23)—are each a dynamic, living function of the very love of God. Each is active, growing, benefiting the life of the believer in whom Christ resides, as well as all those whose lives He touches through that believer.

We only have the fruits of God's Spirit to the extent we have the presence and person of Christ's life within. The degree to which we allow Christ to control all of our character, conduct and conversation will determine the abundance or scarcity of the fruit of His life produced in us.

To put it in the plainest possible terms, *the fruits of the Spirit are the character of Christ made visible in me by His presence at work in me.* It is literally the life of God governing my character, the love of God shown to others through my conduct and conversation.

The actual expression of these fruits in our daily lives stands as the supreme test of whether or not Christ lives in us, filling us for fruit-bearing by His Spirit.

2. The *gifts* of God's Spirit are not indicators of a divine life *within,* as the fruits of the Spirit are. Rather, the gifts are special capacities bestowed *upon* a believer for special service to the church.

The gifts of the Spirit are not an integral part of the character of Christ. Though they can be used to give expression to His work within, they are not an essential part of the love of God. Yet they are sometimes the vehicle used to demonstrate that love. They are not the very life of God's Spirit, but rather the capacity bestowed on a believer to manifest that life.

These "gifts," these capacities for service, are bestowed as a unique responsibility to each Christian to make a valuable contribution to the corporate body of believers. Some gifts are considered by God to be much more useful and more important to the whole Body than others. Some benefit everyone. Others benefit only the recipient. The gifts may or may not be used. Some who have them never discover that they do. They may lie inert for years, unused.

In my case, it was not until I was about 47 years old that it became evident God had given me the gift of teaching. Before that I believed my only gift was "helps."

Lastly, it must be mentioned that these gifts can be misused and abused. They can be exploited by counterfeit forces in the spiritual realm. They can be used to deceive others. They can be employed for destructive ends and selfish personal gratification.

Let us consider now the gift of prophecy. Contrary to what most Christians believe, this "gift" does not deal with just foretelling future events. That is one of its true functions, but its most important role, by far, is the capacity to speak on God's behalf to men. It is the noble ability to take divine, supernatural truth revealed by God and transmit it to human beings. "God, who at sundry times and in divers manners spake in time past unto the fathers by the prophets. . ." (Heb. 1:1).

In God's estimation this is one of the greatest of all gifts. It can be such a great benefit to so many. By it mankind can clearly understand not only who God is, but also what His will and intentions are for His creation.

We are urged to both desire and seek to receive this gift (1 Cor. 14:1). Astonishingly, one seldom hears a Christian pray for this capacity. Most people are paralyzed with apprehension about it. They would rather die than speak out boldly as a prophet for The Lord.

In startling contrast, thousands upon thousands deliberately seek the gift of tongues. Whether through personal ignorance or the persuasion of men, this is not the gift which we are told by the Spirit to desire and seek. Many Christians pray and plead and insist on being given this least beneficial of all capacities, the one which usually edifies only the recipient. Essentially, this becomes a self-centered desire which can provide the enemy with a beachhead of delusion in a life.

We have few prophets of God in our pulpits today. But we do have predators with only the trappings of a prophetic gift, making much of their so-called prophetic utterances. They shout about the frightening future that faces the planet. They play upon the fears and emotions of their audiences. They cater to the insatiable curiosity of the human mind regarding the unknown future. They entertain the masses with their sensational predictions.

But we long for the true prophets of God who in

brokenness of spirit and burning tears of travail call their generation to repentance from sin.

We yearn for modern counterparts to men like Ezra, Elijah, Jeremiah and John, the flaming Baptist. People perish for lack of brave spokesmen prepared to lay down their lives for the sake of God's Word, and God's people, in a wretched world of wickedness.

So the declaration of God's Spirit is stern and severe in this thirteenth chapter: "Though I have the gift of prophecy, but have not the love of God to lay my life down for those I address—it is all of no account" (author's paraphrase).

Spiritual leaders endowed with the great persuasive gifts of prophecy, eloquence and oratorical language need to examine their motives carefully before God. Are they in the pulpit because of its power, its prominence and prestige? Or are they there because they are ready to lay down their very own lives to feed God's flock, to bring the lost and the straying to Christ, The Good Shepherd?

Do they prophesy for personal gain? Or does their proclamation of divine truth come out of hearts consumed with compassion for perishing people?

What is true for our leaders is equally applicable to us, the lay people in the pews. If Christ's Spirit has bestowed upon us this capacity to speak clearly to others regarding God, it should be always in humility, mercy and truth.

We do not prophesy to impress people with our eloquence or persuasiveness. We do not declare God's Good News of salvation to pander to our ego but rather to bring men from death to life, from despair into the wondrous love of God.

One vivid and indelible memory from my early

childhood is bound up with the copious tears shed by my mother and dad in their travail over the tribes-people around them in Africa. They would spend hours on their knees in anguish of spirit over the lost. This travail eventually led to a mighty awakening amongst the Africans. We need that kind of love in our lives, too, whether we are ministering to heathen overseas or reaching out to a next-door neighbor who does not know Christ.

In this verse The Spirit of God also deals with the whole range of knowledge, with mysteries and their understanding. This covers both secular and spiritual education, enlightenment and comprehension. It embraces the entire realm of learning upon which modern man puts so much emphasis. The acquisition of diplomas, degrees and human credentials upon which we put so much store is here put into divine perspective.

He tells us plainly that no matter how great our qualifications, unless accompanied by love, they are of no value. This comes as a rude shock to a world where one's relative worth is often measured by academic credentials or factual knowledge.

Again the classic comparison is made between what is important to man and what is of value to God. Human beings, conditioned by a scientific society that largely ignores God, bases behaviour on the standard of technology and human philosophy.

Christ, on the other hand, calls us to live our lives according to the standards of truth, love and compassion revealed to us in His life and by His Word.

For many this leads to tremendous tension within, "Because the foolishness of God is wiser than men; and the weakness of God is stronger than men" (1 Cor. 1:25).

People do not really believe this concept!

Individuals who for years gladly submit themselves to the demands of their chosen discipline in the arts, humanities, sciences, business or athletics often will refuse to come under the discipline of God's love. They will gladly abide by the standards established in other fields of human knowledge in order to advance, yet they reject the standards of Christ's love as a guide to godliness.

It is ironic that although order, progress and mutual understanding depend on adhering to specific laws and principles in every other area of life, men reject this concept in their code of personal moral conduct. It is as if to say, "In engineering I will abide by the laws of engineering, but in loving either God or man I shall do as I please—each person is a law to himself."

Are we surprised then at the chaos and confusion in human conduct? Are we startled by the selfishness in society? Are we alarmed at the growing anarchy around us?

The love of God, contrary to what most Christians think, is not some sweet, sentimental emotion that seeps into their lives from God's Spirit. The love of Christ is a powerful, profound setting of man's will to do God's will in this wretched world. It is that tough and uncompromising determination of a man's entire soul to submit to God's Spirit in complying with His wishes and carrying out His commands. (Please read John 14, 15 and 16 prayerfully.)

This is the very practical way whereby we demonstrate that we do in actual fact have God's love, "for love worketh no ill to his neighbor: therefore love is the fulfilling of the law" (Rom. 13:10), that is to say, God's wishes.

If a person misses this vital truth he has missed the whole meaning to his existence on the planet. All else is pointless, a mere mockery, for it all passes away.

Finally, God's Spirit, in a single shattering sentence, contrasts faith with love. Again He reveals that even mighty faith sufficient to move mountains is of no worth without love.

This strikes us as an enigma. We of the West put so much emphasis upon a person's capacity to make things happen. We idolize the "doers," the "movers" and "shakers" amongst us. But God does not.

In fact, the use of faith amongst Christians purely for the purpose of self-gratification and self-improvement has become a formidable fad. From pulpits across the country, people are taught that all they need do is "confess it, then possess it." No matter what it is they desire, be it health, wealth, power or pleasure, all of it is available on demand.

The doers, movers and shakers are more preoccupied with what they can claim from Christ than in laying down their lives in service for Him and the suffering around them. In the name of God and with flambouyant faith, mighty miracles are purported to happen. Prophetic utterances are declared. Evil spirits of all sorts are exorcised. Various wonderful and stunning projects are paraded for public view.

Yet the searching question which always must be asked is, "Was this done in selfless, self-giving love in compliance with the will of God, or is it merely the spectacular, selfish aggrandizement of man to flaunt his faith?"

Again, the final criterion is not one of mighty works. It is not a question of achievement or accomplishment. It is not even one of stunning society with the spectacular. Rather the ultimate determination from Christ's viewpoint is, "Was this His will, done in His love, for the sake of others?"

If not, the most grandiose display of faith will be a farce, a show, but nothing more. Though it may produce a measure of self-gratification, that does not mean it satisfies God or brings pleasure to His person. He may even disclaim having any knowledge of the performance. If it was carried out apart from Him, who is love, it is all for naught. (With humility read Matt. 7:21-23.)

4

*"And though
I bestow all my
goods to feed the
poor, and though
I give my body
to be burned,
but have not
love, it profits
me nothing."*

(1 Cor. 13:3, NKJV)

SOCIAL SERVICE WITHOUT GOD'S LOVE

This verse is one of the most difficult to consider. It stands in contrast with the character of Christ, with divine love, because it deals with our human motives. Human nature being what it is in its unregenerate condition, much of that which passes as "charity" in society, though of merit in man's estimation, may be less so in God's economy.

Since the whole question of social service is so much debated in Christian circles, it is vital that we look at it with intense integrity. Always the questions must be asked, "*Why* am I bestowing my goods to benefit the poor?" "*Why* do I involve myself in social service for underprivileged people?"

It is true this type of ministry has been considered one of the main missions of the church. Some groups consider it of greater importance than proclaiming the good news of Christ's redemption. They prefer to feed hungry stomachs rather than hungry spirits. They are quick to cry out for the poor in body, slow to see the need of the poor in spirit.

The Spirit of God speaking here through the Apostle Paul does not specifically define whether the poor are such in their physical needs or spiritual poverty. Nor does it matter. For to minister to either class entails the outlay of time, energy, strength, skill, money and material assistance of one sort or another.

The crucial question is, do I really *love* the poor? Do I truly care with Christ's compassion for those who need to be fed, whether it is earthly or spiritual food?

If not, any activity I may engage in to succour those who are underprivileged becomes an empty endeavour. In fact, though it may benefit the recipient to some degree, it may be pointless and of no profit whatever to me, the donor.

Why? Simply because a great deal of the charity carried out in our culture is done for one of three reasons:

1. As an insidious form of self-satisfaction. Somehow it panders to a personal desire for self-gratification. These people give not because they are deeply concerned about the deprived, but because they just want to "feel good." These are the so-called "do-gooders."

2. To contribute to charity whether for feeding hungry mouths or feeding hungry hearts is too often merely a "sop" to one's conscience. God's Spirit may speak to us to go personally to the poor. But we choose to "go" vicariously through our donations in a detached way. This is much less costly in terms of personal discomfort and involvement.

3. Many give generously to the poor simply to dodge paying excessive taxes. There is virtually no personal concern for the terrible and terrifying plight of the millions who perish in the earth.

We in the Western world have serious and well-nigh insurmountable difficulties in dealing with our "poor." So many forms of social services are available, both in government agencies and church relief programs, many Christians have not encountered personally the earth's truly poor.

I grew up amongst some of the most poverty-ridden people in East Africa. They lived in crude mud huts, barely subsisting on corn meal and bananas. Many were riddled with despicable tropical diseases. They lived at a level of degradation very little above the animals around them. They were plunged in the darkness and despair of spirit worship. Poor, poor people! Hungry for food, hungry for health, hungry for bread from Heaven, hungry for love.

As Dad often said, "You don't just come to such people with the Gospel. You come with bread and cups of cold water in one hand, and the great Good News of Christ's love in the other. You pour out all of yourself to serve the whole man!"

And the only possible motivation that will prompt a person to do this in total, unselfish self-giving is the love of God. It is the unashamed, profound caring for others that characterized the life of Our Lord when He was here amongst us. "And Jesus went about all the cities and villages, teaching in their synagogues, and preaching the gospel of the kingdom, and healing every sickness and every disease among the people. But when he saw the multitudes, he was moved with compassion on them, because they fainted, and were scattered abroad, as sheep having no shepherd" (Matt. 9:35-36).

For those unable to go to the poor in person, it is still possible to express the compelling love of God in very practical ways. One very important key is prayer. It is nearly impossible to pray for someone without loving him. We can pour out our souls in prayers of intercession for the poor; we can pray for those who are ministering to their needs. We can so discipline our own lives in simplicity and moderation that we have an abundance to share with them. We can give and give and give with glad generosity, loving others as God Our Father first loved us.

Living this way, with a vivid impression of the perishing and needy clearly before us, we will be blessed beyond measure. There will flow through us rivers of refreshment, strength and support to a host of materially and spiritually poverty-stricken people to the ends of the earth.

We can be a part of God's great relief plan for the world. It will be a stirring experience to share in lifting the woes of the world. But to do it aright, we must truly care in God's generous way of love for them.

In speaking of giving our bodies to be burned, the Spirit of God is again dealing with the inner motivation for our actions. What prompts me to "burn out" for others? What underlying cause makes a man or woman willing to be made a martyr?

When I was a lad, a phrase often used by Christians but seldom heard today, was, "I would much rather burn out for God than merely rust out!" It sounded very heroic and noble, but I often wondered who the speaker was trying to impress.

In the days during which these profound principles stated in 1 Corinthians 13 were written, it was not uncommon for Christians to be burned at the stake. The formidable price many paid for their confidence in Christ was to be consumed in flames in order to satisfy the evil debauchery of the cruel Romans. Nor across the ensuing centuries has there been any diminution in the ranks of unknown followers of Christ who have been done to death for their faith.

The Spirit of Christ casts no reflection on the brave men and women willing to lay down their lives in martyrdom. Often it is intense persecution of God's people that produces an enormous impetus to the church. Again the issue is one of the purpose behind it all.

Sometimes pagan people and non-Christians deliberately burn themselves up to make a public statement of protest. What sort of statement is the Christian making by his or her "burn out"?

Is this a means of attracting attention to one's self, or is it a genuine willingness to be consumed for others without public recognition?

Are we trying to impress others or to please God?

Do we engage in self-sacrifice for subtle reasons of self-aggrandizement, or are we sincerely concerned for the welfare of our fellows? The line of demarcation between the two is often hazy and sometimes obscured by our own lack of objectivity.

To be honest before God Himself, to be honest with those we serve, and to be honest with ourselves, it is necessary to allow God's Spirit to search our hearts and make clear to us what our motives are.

The tragic truth is that often those we serve can detect more quickly than anyone else whether or not our actions are done in love or not. The unfortunate of the earth have an acute capacity to distinguish quickly between the person who offers them help in a patronizing way and those who come with compassionate love.

The genuine, selfless love of God, active in a person's life, speaks so clearly and with such concern that it is unmistakable. Its winsomeness is louder than any human language. Its warm, transparent integrity surpasses any eloquence. Its wholesome aura transcends any expertise or education.

This quality of love that is prepared to give and give and give to others without any thought of return is a gift from God Himself. It is part of His own life being expressed through the common clay of our humble humanity.

This humble aspect of love which will allow a man or woman to gladly burn out on behalf of others without grudging, in total obscurity if need be, is nothing less than the life of Christ. It comes into our daily conduct as we learn to love others as He first loved us. Such love comes by practice, not by whimsy.

It is an aspect of life which we actually learn from living with Christ. It is a way of life which finds ever increasing expression as He lives out His very life through us.

It is not a matter of theology or doctrine.

It is not a question of biblical knowledge.

It is not the exercise of a gift or gifts.

Rather it is cups of cold water given to the needy with compassion. It is setting the prisoners free with the chain-shattering power of the great Good News of God's love for them in Christ. It is offering comfort, encouragement and a listening ear to those with heavy, pain-filled hearts. It is the clothing of the naked both with apparel to keep out the cold as well as the new garments of the righteous goodness of Our God.

This loving self-giving comes through seven specific steps. Understanding them clearly can transform our lives. Our life with God will become one of enormous benefit to those in physical, material, emotional and spiritual need as well as a benediction to Christ Himself.

Here are the basic principles for learning to love:

1. *We can only learn to love those to whom we have been introduced.*

If we are to care for the poor, we must see them in their poverty. If we are to care for God, we must see and meet Him in Christ (John 14:9).

We do not love—we *cannot* love—the one we have never encountered. Sometimes it requires perseverance, time and effort to meet those whom we will love.

2. *There must be a positive response within the soul and spirit to the one met.*

It has been said that "Our friends were once all strangers." So it is likewise true both with God and man. We must be drawn to those afar off from us.

It is the specific work of God The Holy Spirit to elicit a personal response within our spirits to Christ, and out of that to the poor and needy around us. He it is who quickens our conscience, enlivens our faith and enables us to be drawn to them.

For the fact is, all of us have been strangers to Him. And for many in our affluent western society, the truly poor and bereft of the earth are still unknown strangers.

3. *Having seen and met the Saviour in His Word, through the revelation of the Holy Spirit, or in the poor, we must give them our attention.*

If one is to truly love God or man, neither can be held at arm's length. We must not have a mere nodding acquaintance. We cannot act as mere spectators.

Instead, we find our attention being focused on the newfound friends. We are drawn into the circle of their lives. We are no longer distant and detached.

4. *Our time, our thoughts begin to center on this person to the exclusion of others.*

By the choice of our own wills we begin to spend more and more time in communion with Christ. Out of that relationship we give increasing attention to the needs of others.

In a remarkable manner, other competing interests begin to fade away.

5. *Because of a growing affection and true concern for Christ and His suffering ones, we are prepared to suffer with them.*

It matters not what the price is we are asked to pay, be it in time, strength, labour, money, discomfort or even mortal danger, we gladly give and give and give. This is the laying down of one's life in love for another.

This is the beginning of a valid expression of God's love in our experience. It is the character of Christ in our conduct.

6. *The daily decisions we make to devote ourselves to Christ and to His interests in the earth are evidence of His love in us.*

John, the dearly beloved old Apostle, wrote with such impact, "My little children, let us not love in word, neither in tongue; but in deed [action] and in truth [integrity]" (1 John 3:18).

As we learn to love both Christ and His own children in the earth, that devotion will be much more than mere rhetoric. It will be shown in tears, in toil, in sharing, in giving, in earnest intercession—in a thousand little ways in which we do God's will in this weary world.

7. *As this love is learned in the crucible of life, it is demonstrated with joy and wholehearted delight.*

To love with the love of God is not martyrdom. It is not to feel put upon or exploited. It is not to be deprived of joy. Quite the opposite! For the person who has found that which is much greater than himself, in which to invest all of life, has found the secret to serenity.

The greatest good to which any individual can give his entire being is God Himself, in Christ. And God is love. So to give ourselves to Him is to give ourselves to loving Him, in person and in His people.

Where do we find God? We find Him in Christ. We find Him in the poor, the needy, the lost, the people whom He brings across our path. For by His own definite declaration He has said, *"Inasmuch as you have done it to one of the least of these my brethren, you have done it to me"* (Matt. 25:50).

5

*"Love suffers long
and is kind;
love does not
envy. . . ."*

(1 Cor. 13:4, NKJV)

THE QUALITIES OF CHRIST'S CHARACTER

The process of "learning to love" described in the preceding chapter is of long duration. It does not happen in a single day or overnight. It calls for fortitude, perseverance and endurance over long spans of time. It calls for fidelity in practice and faithful devotion to the object of love that lasts a lifetime.

This principle has been proven over and over again. Whether that which we learn to love is something as exciting as tennis, as stirring as music, as complex as chemistry, as romantic as a life mate, as needy as the poor, or as noble as Our King of Kings, Jesus Christ Himself.

The seven steps set out in the previous pages apply to all of life. A person becomes a fine tennis player, a remarkable musician, a superb scientist, a fine life partner, a wondrous benefactor to the poor, a devoted child of God by patient, and at times painful, perseverance. This is the meaning of long-suffering.

The remarkable point that escapes most people is this: no matter what area of life we are active in, loving demands that we learn to obey the rules and "go by the book." Again, this is as true for music as for God Himself. The path to success and perfection in learning love requires implicit obedience to the laws and principles that govern every sport, art or discipline in life.

Strange as it seems, we humans do not hesitate at all to invest our whole lives in learning to obey the laws of athletics, art or science. Yet we rebel against learning to obey the laws of God for loving Him and for loving others.

There is an amazing statement made by God's Spirit in Hebrews 5:8-9 regarding Jesus Christ: "Though He was a Son, yet He learned obedience by the things which He suffered. And having been perfected, He became the author of eternal salvation to all who obey Him" (NKJV).

Many modern Christians deeply resist the idea that love and obedience are intertwined in our relationship to both God and men. The assertion that these attitudes so inherent in Christ's character should also be a hallmark of a Christian raises inner resistance in the Western mind used to democratic ideas of "freedom" and "doing our own thing." They retort that to so live is to be "under the law," to be legalistic, to be bound.

Yet the answer to all of these charges is simply to read quietly Christ's last great discourse with His disciples in John, chapters 14, 15 and 16. He iterates and reiterates that "if you love me, you will keep my commandments—you will abide in my word—you will do what I direct you to do."

In layman's language, we will learn to love God and man, just as Christ learned it, by obedience and suffering and patient perseverance. We will begin to "go by the book," the Book of Life that contains all the rules necessary for successful loving.

It always astonishes me that men and women who will suffer anything for their love of sport, art, science or success in business refuse to suffer at all in succeeding at love. They flippantly brush off any suggestion that God Himself, who is love, has provided us with a rule Book for learning how to love Christ and man.

It is as if to say, "I will play and live by the rules in every other area of life. But when it comes to love, each of us can do as we wish."

What an absolute absurdity! Are we surprised at the chaos, the confusion in contemporary society? Are we startled by the corruption and degradation in our culture? Are we abashed by the immoral behaviour of some within the Christian community?

The love of God does not give us the freedom to behave as libertines. It calls us to commitment, to live in complete decency and integrity. The laws of God's design demand that we shall care for others and respect others and suffer for others as much as we do for ourselves. (Prayerfully read Gal. 5:13-14.)

This is not easy or comfortable or natural for us to do.

It entails some suffering—long-suffering.

It demands self-discipline under adversity.

Just as He puts up with our perverseness, often Christ calls us to put up with some unlovely characters. He puts us into situations where the only healing that can come to others is through our "putting up with" their wretchedness in long, strong, unshakable suffering.

It will cost something to be *a long-suffering soul.* It costs heartache, grief, inconvenience, disappointment, tears and loneliness to help bear the burdens of this woebegone, tired world.

But if the very life of Christ is at work in us, we will patiently comply with His wishes. We will be closely identified with His interests in society. We will share actively in His long-suffering on this earth. Only thus can the loads of others be lifted in love.

Yet it is essential to point out here that this long-suffering must be endured with kindness, not resentment. We *must* do it with compassion and mercy for lost men!

God's love to us is oh, so kind, so generous, so very merciful, so patient! Where would we be but for the lovingkindness of Christ! What hope would anyone have of Heaven, our Home with Him, were it not for His kind concern?

Without apology I here repeat my own testimony of God's enduring kindness in my own life as stated in my book *A Gardener Looks at the Fruits of the Spirit.*

"His merciful kindness is great toward us" (Ps. 117:2) is a refrain that never dies. It is repeated in the Psalms scores of times as a reminder that the mercy, compassion and kindness of God flow to us freely, abundantly every day in refreshing rivers.

The kindness of God has drawn me to Him with bonds of love stronger than steel. The mercy of my Lord has endeared me to Him with enormous gratitude and thanksgiving. The generous compassion and intimate care of His Gracious Spirit are an enriching refreshment, new every day!

It is extremely difficult to convey on paper in human language the incredible kindness of my Father, God. It seems to me that anyone who attempts to do this falls short. There is a dimension of divine generosity that transcends our human capabilities to clearly convey to one another. It can be experienced, but it cannot be explained.

It is the kindness of God expressed in Christ and revealed to us by His Spirit that supplies my salvation. His kindness makes provision for my pardon from sins and selfishness at the cost of His own laid-down life. It is His kindness that forgives my faults and accepts me into His family as His dearly beloved child. His kindness enables me to stand acquitted of my wrongdoing, justified freely in His presence. God's kindness removes my guilt, and I am at one with Him and others in peace. It is the kindness of God that enables Him to share Himself with me in the inner sanctuary of my spirit, soul, and body. His kindness enables me to be remade, refashioned, re-formed gently into His likeness. His kindness gives enormous meaning and dignity to this life and endless delight in the life yet to come.

As this kindness flows into our lives from the life of Christ, it must in turn be passed on to others around us. It is an integral part of the rivers of refreshment that can spring up from within us to run out and refresh others.

Those whose lives it touches may not always return or reciprocate that love. Some may even spurn it or react in anger as they did with Christ. He warned us it might even mean being hated (John 15:17-19).

The divine principle of sowing and reaping still

applies. In due course we may be sure that others, from whom we never expected it, will show us great kindness. Our God is not only the God of all consolation but also all compensation.

Show kindness and in due time you will receive it back in abundance. Sow a crop of compassion and you will harvest a field of goodwill. He will surprise you with spontaneity and unexpected delight.

Some of the most memorable moments in life can be those flashing interludes when kindness stole softly into our daily round of duty. I call these times "My Master's bonuses." They come as a joyous surprise. They come unannounced. They come to cheer us along our way.

We are also told in our text for this chapter that the "love of God" is not envious. Some modern translations use the word "jealous" instead of envious. That is not quite accurate. There is a subtle but profound difference between envy and jealousy.

One envies that which another achieves or owns. We envy that which does not belong to us. Jealousy, on the other hand, is an inflamed sense of personal possession. It is self-centeredness and self-preoccupation with what I already own and am unwilling to share with others.

Next to the sin of self-pity, which is without doubt the most heinous of all human sins carried out against God by Christians, jealousy is perhaps the next most despicable. Self-pity implies God has failed me and cannot care for me. Jealousy implies that I am so self-centered I cannot share what is entrusted to me.

It is obvious neither attitude ever occurs in the impeccable character of Christ. The statements made in Scripture that God is jealous would be much better translated *zealous*. For example, He is zealous for His name, for His reputation, for His presence amongst His people. Being God very God, supreme and sovereign in the universe, there is no reason He should envy or be jealous of anyone, for He has no equals.

We humans with our limited comprehension of God's character tend to overindulge in anthropomorphism. We attribute qualities of human personality to Him which at times are very erroneous. These are a caricature of His true likeness. To say He is jealous or envious as we are is very misleading and wrong!

On the other hand, the love of God is exceedingly fair, generous and well-intentioned toward others. Christ is delighted when He sees others succeed. He is elated when His people triumph. He loves to know that because of His poured-out life to us we too can enjoy life abundantly.

We never ever see Christ caught up in the wretched, self-centered role of a rival. We do not see Him debasing Himself with envy, ill-will or any hint of personal jealousy. Even when abused and despised by His detractors, He remained silent and refused to respond with railing against railing. (Meditate on 1 Pet. 2:15-25.)

This is the greatness of Our God.

It is the surpassing generosity of His Spirit.

It is the character of Christ unclouded by discord.

Christ calls us, as His followers, to live our lives on this same lofty plane. He sheds His great love abroad in our characters to keep us from getting mired in the cruel criticism and mud-slinging that is all too common in some Christian circles. Too many are envious of the success or blessings or benefits bestowed on their brothers and sisters in God's family.

Instead we should be glad and cheer for those who are doing well. We should rejoice for any ground gained by those who love The Lord. We should thank Our Father for every inch of territory taken by any Christian in his contest with the enemy.

Our Master calls us to be large in spirit. He is delighted to see us become generous and greathearted toward others engaged in the same work we are doing. He is more impressed with our gracious goodwill, expressed in mercy and kindness, than any other impressive sacrifice we may make. "But go and learn what this means: 'I desire mercy and not sacrifice.' For I did not come to call the righteous, but sinners, to repentance" (Matt. 9:13, NKJV).

Why? Simply because the greatest personal sacrifice one can offer to Him or to one's fellowmen is selfless love—a love that smiles when others succeed; a love that cheers when others triumph; a generous love that does not envy or become jealous.

6

**"Love does not
parade itself,
is not puffed up;
does not behave
rudely. . . ."**

(1 Cor. 13:4, 5 NKJV)

THE LOVE OF GOD IS NOT ARROGANT OR ABRASIVE

If anyone had a good reason to be proud, it was Christ!

Pausing but a few moments to consider His great and mighty achievements throughout the universe, we are struck with awe. He is the *Supreme Creator of all*. He is the sublime sustainer of the biota. He controls the cosmos.

Yet, wonder of wonders, He is also our *Suffering Saviour*. He, the *Everlasting God*, was willing to become a babe in Bethlehem, prepared to work as a carpenter in Nazareth, glad to live in poverty and minister to multitudes in humility. By a clear choice of His own will, He determined to go to His death at Calvary to bear the awful burden of sin for us perishing earth people.

This is He who rose in mighty power from the rock tomb, ascending in splendor to His previous position of power. In majesty and power, He has been crowned Monarch of the Eternal Realms—King of Kings—Lord of Lords—Maker of all!

He has no equal!

He has no peer!

He has utter supremacy!

But such majesty, such power and magnificence has never corrupted His character with arrogance. He has never been tarnished with conceit, pride or abrasive behaviour.

His great strength is shown in His incredible gentleness.

His gracious conduct displays His remarkable might.

He is *The Perfect Gentleman* in the truest sense.

It startles us proud, self-centered earthlings to be told by His Spirit that we, too, should have the same humility of heart, the same servant spirit, as our Master. "Let nothing be done through selfish ambition or conceit, but in lowliness of mind let each esteem others better than himself. Let each of you look out not only for his own interests, but also for the interests of others. Let this mind be in you which was also in Christ Jesus" (Phil. 2:3-5, NKJV).

The human mind has enormous problems with this. Our pride asserts itself with formidable energy in the form of self-esteem, self-assertion, self-interest, or self-aggrandizement. It pulses through our souls and surges through our personalities with ferocious power.

From childhood, human pride parades itself in a thousand subtle disguises. It "struts its stuff" with a subversive vanity that feeds on its own deplorable self-importance. It is pandered to in a hundred ways by the corruption of our sophisticated culture and the gross cynicism of our human society.

61

Beginning with the first syllables we learn to speak, "me"—"I"—"mine" become the center of our focus, the circumference of our self-centered interests. From our first faltering steps we are urged by parents, teachers, associates and now even preachers in our pulpits to "stand on our own feet"—"make your own way"—"fight for the top"—"assert yourself"—"become self-sufficient"—"discover your self-identity"—"fulfill yourself."

Modern false teaching by the "predators in our pulpits" asserts that we can demand whatever we wish from God. Though we are but dust and less than dust upon our puny pedestals of pride, we are taught to insist that *we* be served by *The Most High!* (Carefully read Isa. 40:12-26.)

What an affront! What brazenness! What audacity!

Little do most Christians realize that such proud people are actually an abhorrence to God. He resists them! (See James 4:1-10.)

Show me the person who is humble in heart (will), desiring only to do God's bidding, who is contrite in spirit and seeks to comply with Christ's Spirit, and I will show you the individual with whom God loves to reside. "The Lord is nigh unto them that are of a broken heart; and saveth such as be of a contrite spirit. Many are the afflictions of the righteous: but the Lord delivereth him out of them all" (Ps. 34:18-19).

We as His people are not in this world to extract all we can from it for our own ease and selfish ends. Life is not our oyster to pry open and plunder in pride and arrogance. That is the world's gross and deplorable philosophy. But it should not be a Christian's. The world's aim is self-aggrandizement. Christ's aim is service to others.

The two are set in diametrically opposite directions. The powerful stream of Our Father's will at work in the universe flows against the mindset of a society interested only in self-gratification—the so-called "me" syndrome.

Are we surprised that many moderns are so jaded? Are we taken aback by the cynicism of our age? Are we astonished by the weariness and boredom, the general discontent of our generation?

God made us for Himself, to learn to lose ourselves in the majestic grandeur of His incomprehensible greatness. He formed us to be conformed to His image in the pure joy of pouring ourselves out in the stream of His goodwill for the planet. He urges us by His Wondrous Spirit to find our total fulfillment in complete identity with Christ and His cause in the redemption of human society.

We are not here to play our little private games.

We are not here to pass our little lives in pleasure.

We are not here to lounge around in ease and luxury.

We are here to walk humbly with Our Master and, working with Him, see great and wondrous changes wrought in the world around us. Not because we are great Christians, but because He is Our Great God!

How then, one must ask, is a person to become humble in attitude, contrite in spirit, gracious in character? These are valid questions. Our confused world with its twisted emphasis on self-love demands clear, concise answers.

1. *Read the Word of God* intelligently, sincerely and with an open, receptive attitude. Ask Christ to speak truth, life and spirit to you from its statements.

Soon the clear revelation will come to you that, contrary to all you have been taught and told, you are not a "self-made" person. Every faculty you possess of body, person, mind or spirit is a gift from God Our Father. Every capacity you own for life, learning or earning is a direct bequest from above. They are His benefits entrusted to you for a brief sojourn here.

This will pulverize pride and bring a proper perspective into your outlook.

2. Spend days, weeks and months meditating quietly in the four Gospels. *Carefully consider the character and behaviour of Christ* revealed to us there in such clarity.

Think about the life and language of The Master. Make Him your model of behaviour. As you expose yourself to His presence in those pages, there will begin to be a metamorphosis in your own character. We become like those we emulate.

3. *Pray earnestly* that His Gracious Spirit will fill your mind, emotions and will to overflowing. Actually allow Him to have His way and wishes in your life and experience. Submit deliberately to His sovereignty. Comply with His commands. You will be changed into a humble and contrite soul.

The choice is ours whether we shall be haughty, arrogant people or those who walk humbly with The Master. If the former, then we shall have grief and difficulty in our relationship to Our Father. If the latter, we shall enjoy an intimate friendship with Him that far transcends any human companionship. His constant comradeship then becomes our most precious possession on earth.

The person who so lives with Christ does not behave in an abrasive or rude manner. He is courteous and considerate toward others. He does not treat his associates with contempt or disdain.

One aspect of the Christian community which has deeply grieved me is the harsh, tough, worldly way in which so-called Christian business people abuse others. It is as though in the church they are very proper, courteous people, but in their business transactions their behaviour is quite unseemly.

This duplicity of conduct has been a difficult burden to endure in dealing with all sorts of self-styled Christians in nearly half a century of business. The inclination to drive a hard bargain, to pull off a sharp, shady deal, to throw up a smoke screen of excuses to cover injustices has often dismayed me beyond my ability to explain.

So the declaration made here by God's Spirit is not just some super-spiritual hypothesis. It is the plain statement of practical truth applied to our very ordinary lives. We are to be polite people who deal with others in decency, integrity and courtesy.

Often the world puts Christians to shame in this regard. Some of them are far more considerate and courteous than their Christian counterparts.

Therefore the question has to be asked, "How does a Christian come to have the character of Christ in the rough and tumble of the business community?" We cannot claim to be God's people, yet live as speckled birds, spattered with the world's ways. The excuse will not do that it is a rough world and the only way to survive in the jungle of commercial competition is by being tough.

The basic truth is we must be transformed people (Rom. 12:1-2). We have to become those who allow Christ to control us. Not just in the area of our spirits, but also in the whole realm of our persons—our minds, our emotions and our wills. It is a case of actually being converted in *the way we think* so we come to have the mind of Christ. It means being transformed in our emotional responses so we react to others as Christ does. It involves a profound capitulation of our wills to the control of Christ so that our deepest decisions are in accord with His will and wishes.

All of these principles for proper living have been dealt with in detail in my book *Walking with God.*

Of course none of this will ever happen unless we see ourselves as we are and decide we need to change. So much of the preaching handed out in our pulpits today is like dishing up pablum to pacify irritable children. Most pastors and ministers are too intimidated by the seemingly successful, tough business people in their churches to ever warn them of their wrongdoing. They are too timid to call a spade a spade or bad behaviour what it is—a sin against both God and men.

If indeed the love of God indwells us, we will not exploit other people, even when there is a chance to do so. We will not take undue advantage of our business associates in our transactions. We will not be rude and demeaning to those we consider less privileged or less "sharp" than we are.

This is a difficult order to fill in the setting of a

society that pressures us to push for the top of the heap; that is drunk with the "success syndrome" measured only in dollars, sales and profit sheets; that shouts at us to be first and foremost, while all the time Christ insists it is best to be last.

Again, the choice is ours as to what our conduct will be. So many who appear so placid in the church, so affectionate to their families, are "tough tigers" in the concrete jungles of our business communities. This is no credit to them. Nor should pastors be afraid to tackle this dichotomy in their congregations.

As Christ's followers, our characters should be above reproach. We cannot claim to be Christians and behave like brutes. For the love of God does not behave unseemly. It behaves like a gentleman and a gentle lady—always!

7

"[Love] seeketh
not her own,
is not easily
provoked,
thinketh no evil."

(1 Cor. 13:5)

CHRIST'S CHARACTER IS FREE OF GUILE, IRRITABILITY AND MALICE

Love does not demand its own way!

What an astounding statement! So simple to say. So difficult for us to do. So characteristic of Christ!

This concept diametrically cuts across all our self-centered concepts of what constitutes complete and full achievement. It smashes into atoms all our vaunted human vanity of total self-realization. It is the spear plunged into the heart of our egocentric preoccupation.

These words embody the true meaning of the cross in the life of the Christian.

Unless we clearly understand this idea, there will be a never-ending controversy in our relationship to God Our Father. We will have conflict with Christ Himself. There will be inner subversion against The Spirit of God who endeavours to guide us.

In our arrogance most of us are very sure we know what is best for us. We too often choose our own tangled way through life. We insist on achieving our own ends.

Then we wonder why our lives become snarls from

which only God Himself can extricate us. Oh, such awful agony we endure because of our own self-willed behaviour! What wasted years we forfeit chasing rainbows of our own devising, goals that have no end but an emptiness that mocks us!

The simple truth is we do not know what way is best for us. Only God does. The sooner we agree to follow in His footsteps, the sooner our grief ends. "There is a way which seemeth right unto a man, but the end thereof are the ways of death" (Prov. 16:25).

The "death" spoken of here is not only that of ultimate despair or defeat, but also ultimate alienation from Christ who all along has our best interests in mind. He constrains us to come to Him and live new lives, set free from the fretful pursuit of self-fulfillment. But we resist His overtures. We resist self-abasement. We repudiate the idea of giving up our own ideas.

It all goes against the grain of our contemporary lifestyle.

We insist we will be our own boss.

We demand our own desires.

And the startling, sobering, terrible truth is God will let you go on your own. He will grant you your own selfish wishes. He will never override your will or impose His lofty, noble life upon you. Ultimately, it is your choice at which level and in what way your few years on earth will be spent.

Israel insisted on her own decision not to enter Canaan, the Land of Promise. So for forty years this obstinate nation wandered in the wilderness and perished in the desert wastes.

Israel insisted on having her own king rather than

submit to the monarchy of Jehovah. So they were given Saul and all his terrible, tragic acts.

Yes, God will give you what you insist on. One reaps what is sown. It can be His good and gracious goodwill or it can be our own tragic way.

Christ chose always to do The Father's will. He chose always to do His work. He chose always to speak His words, no matter the cost. The end was total triumph.

The same opportunity is open to us.

Love does not demand its own rights.

We of the Western world with our powerful and often repeated emphasis on the democratic rights of our people have enormous problems here. We insist that as free citizens of the community we have, under our constitution, certain inalienable rights. We call these civil rights.

It is a very ancient tradition, well-nigh sacred to the British people and passed along to their American cousins, that a man's home is his castle. Within the sanctuary of his own domicile he enjoys enormous personal privileges which no one can invade or violate with impunity.

So it is natural for us to jealously guard our own rights. In fact most of us, either consciously or subconsciously, have acquired a fortresslike mentality about standing on our own authority. Like the tough Texas motto symbolized by a coiled rattlesnake ready to strike, we warn others *"Don't tread on me!"*

The net result is a people bent on striking out at any intruder. We are a nation quick on the trigger, fast on the draw. Only now in our more "civilized" era, it is done more often through endless lawsuits and formidable litigation.

So it comes as a shock to be told that Christ did not live that way. It is noteworthy that when He was taken prisoner by the mob on the Mount of Olives, then charged before a kangaroo court, He never once asked for the services of an attorney. He never resorted to revenge. (Read 1 Pet. 2:18-25.)

No, He did not insist on His own rights.

And if in truth His life is real in us, neither will we.

Rather we will believe implicitly that Our Father, in His own good way, will settle the scores of life with justice.

My personal testimony here is that He has proven Himself utterly reliable in this way all my life. Put in colloquial terms, "He laughs best who laughs last." Let God be your judge. Let Him settle the scores. Give Him your rights even in the small issues of life. This is the path of serenity of soul.

Love does not insist on its own aims and aspirations.

If we are going to have great ambitions in life, let them be of The Master's arrangement. God Our Father gives us great dreams. His Vital Spirit can impart to us stirring visions of what His best intentions are for us.

May they not be our own design.

The person caught up in the great, ongoing purposes of God for the planet knows and senses the thrill of living and moving in God's will. It is not a hardship to endure. It is a dynamic stimulation of spirit. Our motivation is not self-interest but enormous gratitude to God for sharing His wonderful generosity with us mere mortals.

We can love in His way and live in His way, only because He loved us this way first and now lives in us this way.

His aims become ours. His ambitions become ours. His name and reputation are at stake in us. His love is on the line. Let us live up to His noble standards, yet in lowliness of attitude.

Love is not easily provoked.

It is the haughty spirit, the arrogant soul obsessed with its own ways and wishes that is readily aroused. Anger flashes out at any adversary. Temper rises to react to any transgression against its owner. Belligerence breaks out in angry provocation against any opponent.

For lack of a better description, I have called such proud individuals, *porcupine people.* Every deadly quill is tense and ready to impale those who dare to endanger its self-interests.

Quick temper is an attitude passed over too often as being of no great consequence. Actually it is a most serious evil in the disposition. It not only blights the character of the one who is angry, but casts gloom and injury over those who feel its wrath.

There is a place, and there are appropriate times, when Christians should express rightful indignation over wrongs done to others. We are too often silent when we should stand and shout for justice to be done to others.

But angry outbursts of abuse against associates to express hurt over our own interests have no helpful role in our conduct. They shame us. They becloud cordial relationships. They tend to alienate even those who might excuse us.

As a young man I had a terrifying, hair-trigger temper. It would erupt in devastating violence like an unpredictable volcano blowing its top. At times even I was alarmed by the horrendous heat of my awful anger. It would convulse my whole person, body, mind and spirit in ferocious fury.

At the age of 27 I read Henry Drummond's classic essay, "Ill Temper." For the first time I saw what my anger really was. It drove me to my knees before Christ in contrition. In His gracious way His Spirit flooded into mine to flush out the filth and pollution of a soul stained with "self-righteous rottenness."

Here are excerpts from Professor Drummond's remarkable insights:

"Jealousy, anger, pride, uncharity, cruelty, self-righteousness, sulkiness, touchiness, dog-gedness, all mixed up together into one—ill temper.

"It is the intermittent fever which tells of un-intermittent disease; the occasional bubble escaping to the surface, betraying the rottenness underneath.

"One of the first things to startle us about sins of temper is their strange compatibility with high moral character."

If we are to be truly Christ's people, we cannot endure such contamination of our character. We must be put right within by His righteousness. We must be cleansed by His incoming. We must be purified by the presence and power of His Wholesome Spirit.

There is no other way.

It is the expulsive, explosive newfound power of His love flooding into our experience that can expel the debris of our own desires. And this Christ does for the one who wants it to happen.

Love thinketh no evil.

An entire chapter could be devoted to this one phrase.

Its standards are so high. Its values are so lofty. Its motives are so pure. This is the love of God, the attitude of Christ, the stance of His own sweet Spirit.

How completely opposite from our own perverse outlook on life! Too often we see only the mud, not the sunshine after the showers. We too frequently find fault instead of looking for the lovely. We too easily are suspicious and cynical instead of being bouyant with good cheer. Our minds are clouded with evil intentions when they could sing with innocence.

Oh, that our inner attitudes were as gracious as God's! "For I know the thoughts that I think toward you, saith the Lord, thoughts of peace, and not of evil, to give you an expected end" (Jer. 29:11).

Being a very practical man, I have come to the conclusion that in large part a person's thoughts are the product of his intellectual diet. We simply reflect back that to which we expose our minds. If we feed on filth and falsehood that pours from the media and corrupt culture of our generation, we will think in evil terms.

If we choose corrupt companions, associate with perverted minds, absorb lustful lyrics, read passionate literature, watch suggestive television programs, accept deceptive human philosophy from our schools and universities, and allow materialism to mesmerize our minds, we will become persons with wicked intentions.

It is a simple, straightforward equation, "As he thinketh in his heart, so is he" (Prov. 23:7).

The alternative is a deliberate choice on the part

of the Christian to develop a pure and wholesome outlook on life. As we set our wills deliberately to do this, God's Spirit will honour our decision to devote ourselves to that which is noble and great. He will actually *work in us* to will and to do of His own good pleasure.

Spend time in the Scriptures. Get into good books. Learn to appreciate fine music. Relish great art and participate in it. Make friends with true Christians— noble, loyal people. Enjoy the beauty of trees, flowers, fields, sea and sky. Look for the strength and goodness in others. Give hearty thanks to God for all the joys of life. (Read Phil. 4:4-9.)

In His wondrous love Christ will change your character as you continually expose yourself to companionship with Him. You will begin to see the touch of His presence in all the world around you. You will become beautiful in your heart and mind.

Give generous gratitude for His grace and love that allow you to live and move and have your very being in Him.

8

*"[Love] rejoiceth
not in inquity,
but rejoiceth in
the truth."*

(1 Cor. 13:6)

GOD'S LOVE
FINDS JOY
ONLY IN TRUTH

For the earnest Christian, the sixth verse of this "Love Chapter" of the New Testament is one of the most important in all of God's Word. It goes to the very heart of the issue, *Where lies joy?*

The Spirit of The Most High, speaking to men across the great spans of human history, speaking through the prophets and apostles of His own choice, speaking directly to us through the life and teaching of Our Lord Jesus Christ Himself, refers constantly to the "joy of the Lord."

The oft-reiterated theme of "rejoicing" is one of the great hallmarks of the life of God Himself. Our Father by special revelation shows us that His character is distinguished by joy. He assures us again and again in scores of scriptures that it is possible for God's dear people to be impelled and sustained by His unique joy. We are urged and encouraged always to find our joy in Him, who is love.

If we are to understand this joy of the Lord, the joy in the Holy Spirit, as it is sometimes called, we must first see how it relates to happiness.

The word "happy" as used in God's Word was originally an ancient Anglo-Saxon word which meant "fortunate" or "well-favored." For example, "Happy is that people, whose God is the Lord" (Ps. 144:15).

Unfortunately some modern translations of the Word of God have interchanged joy and happiness rather freely. This is a grievous error, for they are not the same.

In its modern understanding, happiness is very much a worldly word. It is a passing, transient sensation that depends upon what is "happening" around a person. It has to do with the people, events or circumstances that touch our lives from outside.

If my family is fond of me, if my friends are loyal, if my associates are faithful, I can be happy. If not, I may well be in deep distress.

If my health is flourishing, my career is prospering, and I am financially secure, I may be happy. But if the opposite happens I may be very unhappy.

If people or circumstances make possible the acquisition of special little gifts or delights which bring personal pleasure, I may be happy with them for a few hours. But if I am bereft of any or all, I may feel unhappy.

This simply is not the equivalent of joy.

Yet increasingly the modern-day church aims toward happiness; it has allowed the world's value system of happiness to become equated with God's unique attribute of joy. It promotes human happiness as an end in itself to be sought by souls really looking for fulfillment in joy.

The result has been chaos and confusion in the lives of many Christians. For, to be very blunt, to look only for happiness in life is to look for the same thing the world looks for so intently. And because happiness is based on transient things, it can never satisfy the eternal spirit of man.

The classic proof of this can be found in the gloomy disillusionment of millions of successful people who have attained every aim and ambition in life only to be mocked by all they attained. They dreamed they would find joy and satisfaction only to discover all their aspirations turned to dust and ashes. They had missed the mark in life!

This was true in my own career as a young man. By the time I was forty every goal I had ever set myself had been gained, every ambition had been attained, every dream had been fulfilled. Yet I was an empty shell of a man, knowing full well that the achievements of my own selfish aspirations had brought no lasting joy.

Why? Because, like uncounted millions of other human beings, I had been deluded to believe the dreadful, ultimate deception that joy could be found in loving the transient elements of earth's short sojourn. It cannot! It never will be! This is the great delusion under which men apart from God struggle and strive, all for naught. It is the terrible evil which our enemy, Satan, has perpetrated on the planet. It is the awful iniquity of the ages which has led billions of blinded, deceived souls to end up in utter despair.

This is the dilemma of the human race.

This is the paradox of life itself.

This is the mystery of iniquity.

What we thought could bring joy brought sorrow.

What we deemed to be success is but sadness.

What we supposed we owned had become our cruel master.

So men and women stand shattered, bewildered and lost.

In the midst of man's mayhem and confusion, Christ comes to us and declares boldly: "Your life does not consist in the abundance of things you possess" (Luke 12:15, author's paraphrase). (Read also Luke 12:13-21.)

The love of God as seen in the life of Christ makes no attempt whatever to find its fulfillment in loving the passing pleasures of the earth scene. It does not, *cannot,* rejoice in the iniquity of deception and disillusionment perpetrated on the planet by the "god of this world" and the gross folly of human philosophy.

The character of Christ is grounded in the unchangeable goodness of God. It is founded on the eternal faithfulness of Our Father. It is based on the enduring reliability of His mercy, love and justice.

These indestructible, unshakable qualities in the life of God Himself are the eternal ground of all joy. The tremendous truth which seems to escape most Christians completely is that this unique disclosure comes only from Christ. It simply cannot come from man, the world or any other spirit beings.

He and only He is truth. Without apology He stated emphatically, "I am the way, the truth, and the life. No man cometh unto the Father, but by me" (John 14:6).

And that quality of joy which transcends the turmoil of our times, which stands calm and sure when all else is shaken around us, which reposes in strength and surety amid the disasters of our days, is founded in Our Father's love. The eternal truth that He is ever with us, enfolding us in His wondrous care is the ground of our joy.

This is the stirring truth that makes our spirits sing in the darkest night. This love of God for us is the unshakable truth that enables us to face the greatest frustrations with firm courage. This love of Christ empowers us to carry on no matter what calamities cross our paths.

Oh, the unchanging, unshakable stream of God's love that without diminution flows to us from the unbounded fountain of His own wondrous person and life! It has its source in Him. It finds its true fulfillment not in the world nor in men's ways, nor in the transient scenes of time, but in the truth that He is with us, His people, calling out a chosen church, bringing sons and daughters to the full glory of His own character.

This is the great ongoing purpose of Our God.

This is the eternal project He has for the planet.

This is the supreme truth in which both He and we rejoice. (Read Eph. 1:3-10, Phillips.)

This is the love of God finding full expression in a joy that sees common men and women changed into the very likeness of Our Lord. This steady transformation becomes actual reality in the daily experiences of God's children.

This joy does not lie in possessions, achievements, accomplishments, fame, success, wealth or health. This joy resides in that wondrous, indescribable relationship of knowing God as Father, of knowing Christ as Friend, of knowing The Holy Spirit as Constant Companion through all of life. *Oh, what joy!*

Just as a giant gyroscope, whirling silently deep in the center of an ocean liner provides stability in stormy seas, so our joy in God's love for us gives us serenity in the stresses of our days. The profound inner assurance "I am His and He is mine" brings surety and repose in the storms of life.

Turning briefly now to the broader world view, it is important to see the distinction drawn here by The Spirit of God. He recognizes clearly that the vast majority of human society does delight in iniquity, does rejoice in evil. He faces the fact that we live on a planet where wrongdoing and selfish behaviour is the accepted way of life for multitudes. The "fun thing" is to taunt that which is righteous, to scorn that which is gracious and noble.

In a word, the world loves what is wrong.

It does not naturally rejoice in what is right.

It prefers deception to truth.

So the Christian is confronted with hard choices.

We simply cannot love the world and revel in its wicked ways and also claim to love Christ who embodies all truth.

John the beloved Apostle was very plain about this. "Love not the world, neither the things that are in the world. If any man love the world, the love of the Father is not in him" (1 John 2:15).

This does not imply that as God's people we are to be dour and dull, finding no delight in the experiences of life. Quite the opposite! As we view life through the perspective of Christ's life within us, we see living evidence of the truth that His wondrous love is everywhere at work in the world, not just in us.

We rejoice in the astounding beauty of mountains, oceans, forests, fields, birds on wing, flowers open to the sun and ten thousand other touches of His integrity and creativity in the earth. We rejoice in the grandeur of His grace and mercy and truth at work upon the spirits and souls of stubborn, wayward men. We rejoice in the strength of character and honesty of life displayed by His own followers determined to live for Him at any cost.

Yes, oh, yes indeed, the tremendous thrust of the truth as it is in Christ is very much at work in this sin-weary world. And we who claim His name, who are being conformed to His character, who are urged and motivated by His life and love find enormous joy in aligning ourselves with His way, His truth, His life.

The odds against us may be staggering.

To stand for truth may be to stand against the surging current of corruption that swirls around us.

To revel in what is right may be to invite the contempt and ridicule of the majority.

To be the purveyors of God's love and honesty may be to suffer loss and endure hardship in our society.

So what? Did not The Master carefully alert us to the cost of walking in His way? Did He not tell us only a few would choose this path through life?

We are not permanent residents of the planet. We are pilgrims passing through, headed for home. May our steps never become mired in the mud of the world's wretched paths. We *can* travel the high road of excellent, righteous conduct. Living in truth and integrity we can spend our few short years here in joy, love and laughter. Our pure delight is walking with Our Father's hand upon us all the way.

9

"[Love] *beareth*
all things,
believeth all
things, hopeth
all things,
endureth
all things."

(1 Cor. 13:7)

THE LOVE OF GOD ENDURES ALL THINGS IN HOPE

We are startled by this categorical statement that God's love is so majestic it is unbreakable. The character of Christ is so strong it can withstand any shock. The life of God is so grounded in hope that it outlasts every situation in radiant optimism.

Placed at the very end of this remarkable chapter is a second supporting statement: "And now abide faith, hope, love, these three; but the greatest of these is love" (1 Cor. 13:13, NKJV).

In the church literally thousands of messages are given on the subject of God's love. Almost as many are delivered on faith in the life of the Christian. Yet, hope is scarcely ever mentioned, except maybe occasionally at funerals.

I recall, on several occasions, asking congregations if they had ever heard an entire message on "Hope." To my surprise only one or two people could ever recall such a sermon.

This is doubly surprising since God's Word makes clear to us that just as He is the God of all joy, so likewise He is the God of all hope. In fact, His forbearance with us fallen men, His patient endurance with our perverseness, His deep belief that we can become *the children of God*—all are grounded in this remarkable quality of *hope* which is uniquely His.

Unfortunately for all of us moderns the word hope, like the word love, has changed in its meaning across the centuries. It no longer has the same strong basis in reality as it did when first spoken to the church at Corinth under the unction of God's Spirit.

Today in the English language we flippantly and rather facetiously use the word in a casual form—*hopefully*. Hope in this sense merely implies wishful thinking. One supposes something might possibly happen. It carries the vague impression that one might assume something to be so without really being sure.

In this subtle and insidious way, the strength, power and might of this remarkable word *hope* has been eroded away. This is a tragic loss for Christians.

Hope, from God's perspective and in the clear context of Christ's character, is the exact opposite of the indecisiveness described above. *Hope in God is as unshakable as rock.*

It means absolute assurance.

It implies utter confidence in Christ's own impeccable character.

It denotes composed stability and strength in any situation no matter how drastic.

It is overwhelming optimism in the darkest hour.

All of this energy is grounded in the eternal goodness of God Himself. It flows to us from the impeccable character of Christ. It stands sure in the power and person of His Wholesome Spirit.

Hope is the antithesis of despair. It is that quality of God's life available to us which dispels the darkness of the world around us. It is that assurance which enables us to bear any difficulty, which empowers us to believe the best in any situation, which helps us to transcend the strain of our times no matter how difficult they are to endure.

Yet all of this is predicated upon us drawing upon the very life of God that flows to us in a constant stream from Christ. I sometimes refer to this as the Christian's "inner stream." It is that very outpouring of God's love to us by His own Spirit that makes real in us His own life.

The non-Christian knows nothing about this inner life of serene hope that is hidden from view in the character of Christ. He has never tasted the thrill or known the delicious delight of having quiet confidence in Christ. Even though the pennies in his pocket may bear the motto "IN GOD WE TRUST," it really means nothing of spiritual significance to him as a person.

Actually almost the same may be said for most people found in the pews of the church every Sunday morning. For the moment difficulties arise or disaster threatens, they do not hope in God. Rather they immediately seek help from their bankers, lawyers, doctors, business associates, or other professional people who can "hopefully" deliver them from their dilemma.

God calls us to live our lives in a different dimension from that of the world around us. He quietly invites us to find our hope in Him. He urges us to plunge into the inner stream of His life, there to find the help and wholeness we need amid our distress. Our hope should be in God, not in man.

To help us understand this, His Gracious Spirit has given us a vivid word picture in Psalm 42 which portrays a hunted deer in distress and how it finds hope.

Next to Psalm 23, Psalm 42 is, beyond doubt, my favourite. It opens with an arresting cameo of exquisite poetry: "As the hart panteth after the water brooks, so panteth my soul after thee, O God" (v. 1).

A magnificent stag, a buck deer, pursued in the hunt, flees for safety to the hidden mountain streams. Pressed for its very life, it plunges into the surging current of the stream to survive.

The poem concludes with the shout of assurance, the challenging cry of one who has overcome, "Why art thou cast down, O my soul? and why art thou disquieted within me? hope thou in God: for I shall yet praise him, who is the health of my countenance, and my God"! (v. 11).

In the days of David and Solomon, the countryside of Israel was very unlike what it is today. It was terrain covered with lush vegetation, flourishing forests on the hills, and singing streams that flowed from the high country.

There was a large wildlife population. Deer were abundant, both red deer (roe deer) and fallow deer. The latter are now virtually extinct. But at the period in history when the Psalms were composed, venison was a favourite dish. In fact, King Solomon insisted that it be served at his royal table every day (1 Kings 4:23).

So deer hunting was common. The quarry was

pursued by dogs, driven into nets, hunted with bows and arrows, or pursued on horseback to be killed with spears and swords. This Psalm portrays a hunted hart fleeing for its life, seeking safety in the swift-flowing coolness of a mountain stream. Deer—all deer, no matter what species—seek water to survive.

The reader may not realize the size and extent of the deer family worldwide. The largest are the moose, elk and caribou of North America. Then there are the various species of mule deer, black tail deer, white tail deer and others native to Europe and Asia. They all love water. They are all strong swimmers. They all frequent streams, rivers and lakes for safety.

I have watched moose plunge into roaring rivers in the northern Rockies to escape predators. I have seen elk and deer swim across lakes to evade wolves and coyotes. I have observed bucks wounded in hunting rush for the nearest stream.

Why? Why run to water? Why plunge into the flowing current? Why is this their hope of survival?

There are four reasons. Each of the four has an exact counterpart in our lives as God's people. These are precise parallels which can give us great hope in God.

1. *Plunging into the stream provides immediate safety from the pursuer.*

The deer is very familiar with every foot of its own home territory. This includes every water course. It knows every pool, every riffle, every expanse of water that provides protection.

The predator does not. The pursuer will pull up short at the water's edge. Here is a foreign element. Here are deep running currents and rushing waves that spell safety for the deer but imminent danger for the hunter (Ps. 42:7).

Likewise in the life of the Christian, there are times when we feel the very hounds of hell are upon our heels. We feel harried and driven by events over which we have no control. There seems, at times, no place to turn, no spot to escape the onrush of the enemy of our souls.

But there is! There is a place of safety! There is sure hope! That spot of quiet help is in the inner stream of Christ's life flowing to you, around you, over you.

Plunge into His very presence. Immerse yourself in Him. Surge buoyantly into the swift-flowing, deep, still waters of His love that flow to you so freely.

The sure, serene rest and repose that will come to you from Him is, *"All is well."*

2. *Plunging into the stream cools and calms the panting, heated deer.*

Because deer do not have sweat glands to cool the body as some animals do, they have to pant through their open mouths, the same as dogs. Consequently, deer when pursued, quickly become overheated and dehydrated.

The cooling effect of a stream or lake quickly restores the animal's composure and normal body temperature. Almost immediately it dispels its panic and dissipates its frantic fear.

The same is true for us when we come to Christ in our emergencies. Amidst the continuous pressures of our artificial "pressure-cooker" society, there is real repose in the constant love of Our Lord.

Speaking from firsthand experience, I am not

ashamed to say that again and again I come to Christ and literally fling my whole being into His embrace.

It is He who can cool the fever of our furious lives. He can restore serenity to our souls. He can give hope amid our hurried days.

3. *Plunging into the stream slakes the deer's thirst and refreshes its life.*

It is from the stream that the deer must drink. Here its thirst is quenched. Here the body fluids are restored. Here there is beautiful refreshment that brings repose.

Some of us know the fierce and burning thirst that has driven us to seek God. No other source of drink could satisfy the inner yearning that shriveled our spirits and scorched our souls. Empty, parched and dry, we wandered in a wasteland of despair until we came to the river of life that flows to us from Christ. Oh, the refreshment of His life! Oh, the delicious delight of His love streaming to us!

To whom else shall we go? *Thou hast the words of life!* And therein lies our satisfaction. We drink deeply from that inner spring and we live!

He is our hope, always!

4. *Plunging into the stream erases every scent, every spoor, every hint of the past.*

In this way the predator is thrown off the track. He gives up the hunt. His prey escapes in the swift-flowing current of the stream.

Likewise with us as God's children. We can plunge freely into the current of cleansing, forgiveness and full acceptance that flows to us from Christ. It is His deepest desire to wash away the spoor, the tangled tracks, the guilt of all that has gone before. He removes our sins from us, washing them away into the sea of His forgetfulness.

No longer can the enemy pursue us from the past. No longer can he harry us with his charges of wrongdoing.

We have found our hope in God. Our souls are at rest. Oh, the love of God!

In the midst of the stresses and strains of our earth days, there remains this inner stream of the life of God flowing to us in abundant hope. Come to Him often, come to Him daily, to endure and bear with all of life in buoyant optimism. Christ is here. All is well. I am made whole. He is the very health of my countenance amid life's hardships.

Bless His name forever!

10

*"Love never fails.
But whether there
are prophecies,
they will fail;
whether there are
tongues, they will
cease; whether
there is knowledge,
it will vanish away."*

(1 Cor. 13:8, NKJV)

THE CHARACTER OF CHRIST IS CONSTANT— HIS LOVE NEVER FAILS

No other quality in the character of Christ elicits our awe or stabilizes our souls in the same way as His constancy. It is the remarkable consistency of His conduct that makes Him stand out as a symbol of strength and integrity above the chaos of human history.

All around us the earth scene is one of never-ending confusion, change and calamity. Civilizations emerge, rise and then collapse. Human society stumbles along from failure to failure. The best-laid plans of governments fail. The sophisticated schemes of economic well-being fail. The hopes of nations and people fail. All is change, all is in flux, all is in transition and turmoil.

Amid the ruins, in great, unchanging consistency, Christ stands serene and sure and unfailing. Oh, the majesty of The Monarch of the Universe! Oh, the grandeur of Our Lord! Oh, the splendor of Heaven's Royal Sovereign!

What assurance He brings to our spirits. What

calm repose He bestows upon our souls. What sure strength He injects into our puny lives. He does not fail! He cannot fail! He *will not* fail His followers!

This basic truth should put steel in our spines. It should put fire in our faith. It should put peace in our hearts.

Even in the privacy of our personal lives we are, apart from Christ, confronted with never-ending change. Our physical well-being rises and wanes. Our families come, then pass on. Our financial affairs are ever in flux. Friends share our brief life sojourn, then fade away. Deterioration and depreciation erode and destroy our goods and possessions. We discover everything is subject to failure. Even churches rise, flourish and then fall.

So life is ever an increasing challenge to adapt to change. The tension of our times is one of adjusting to a world void of stability. As Our Lord put it, sufficient to each day is the trouble that comes with it (Matt. 6:34).

It has been said facetiously that the only two sure things in life are death and taxes. Actually this is not true. Both Enoch and Elijah bypassed death, and for those who remain at Christ's return, with hope in Him, there will be no death.

As for taxes, many primitive societies simply do not have them. Neither is this form of levy required from the poor even in our own country.

No. The only two sure things in the universe are "change," which happens again and again, and God Himself.

It is to these that man must make some sort of essential adjustment. The changes and fluctuations of the earth scene are at best temporary. The character of Christ never alters. The glory of God, which is of course the splendor of His person, never fluctuates. The inherent love of His Spirit of goodwill to us men never diminishes.

It is only as we open our own souls to Him and receive His as Heaven's Royalty can we ever hope to share that same enduring quality of His constant care.

The Word of God is very clear and specific about the constancy of Christ's character. If we read the Psalms in a modern translation, it is astonishing to discover how the consistency of God's conduct and love is their main theme throughout.

Here are several categorical statements from other portions of Scripture:

"I am the Lord, I change not" (Mal. 3:6).

"And, thou, Lord, in the beginning hast laid the foundation of the earth; and the heavens are the works of thine hands: they shall perish; but thou remainest; and they all shall wax old as doth a garment; and as a vesture shalt thou fold them up, and they shall be changed: but thou art the same, and thy years shall not fail" (Heb. 1:10-12).

"Jesus Christ the same yesterday, and today, and for ever" (Heb. 13:8).

Thus it comes home to us amid the changing scenes of our days that here is One who endures, One who can be counted on always, One who ever remains truly steadfast.

Wonder of wonders, this applies not only to our

fleeting few years upon the planet but also beyond them into the long avenues of eternity that stretch out before us. This thought, this hope, stirs me to the depths. There is no other concept which gives such dignity to me as an individual. "I am His and He is mine forever." No other truth can so encourage a man or woman to face the unknown future as this: *Christ is here. He never changes. He never fails.*

Oh, what a consolation to His children!

Oh, what an encouragement to His people!

Oh, what a stronghold for our faith, feeble as it may be, for it is grounded in His total integrity!

For in essence, when a man truly has God in all His goodness, it matters not what fails around him.

As Paul put it, "I count all things but loss for the excellency of the knowledge of Christ Jesus my Lord" (Phil. 3:8).

It is this awareness of Christ, His very presence pressing in upon us, His love being disbursed to us as a divine dynamic, His character impinging upon our characters, which changes us.

We are, in our humanity, actually changed and remade from our character to His character, from glory to glory, by the influence of The Spirit of God (see 2 Cor. 3:17-18).

So it is that we in some small, feeble, yet shining way become reflectors of His life. We in turn show something of the constancy of God's love to a sickly world. We become in effect candles of hope and light and good cheer in the darkness all around us.

There will be about us a quality of credibility that does not fail. We will be people who are truly consistent in our conduct. We will carry out our commitments to others and to God. We will refuse to fail those who trust us. We will become disciplined individuals of bold courage on whom others can rely. We will be strong enough in Christ to carry on even when *we* don't feel like it. We will not fail to live in dignity and decency. We will be people of our word who bear the name of Christ without fanfare, but in great honour.

Those within the church who claim to be born again and filled with God's Spirit should be totally different from their worldly counterparts. In their conduct and conversations there should be an element of decency, integrity and reliability not found in a society that fails to exhibit these qualities.

God is not impressed by people who pompously boast of being spiritual while behaving like the world. He is calling out of human society, with all of its gross corruption and fallibility, an unusual, special people to be known for their incorruptibility. He is looking for Christians who have the very character of Christ displayed in their deportment.

It is a high calling.

It is a noble life He sets before us.

It is an enormous honour to walk worthy of Him.

Unless a man or woman comes to feel comfortable in the select company of Christ here on this earth, it is not the least likely that they would ever be at ease with Him in the expanses of eternity.

It is sheer humbug to hope that one will be contented with conditions in Heaven if one has never been accustomed to keeping company with Christ here. And a large part of this preparation is learning the utter integrity of the love of God.

We cannot manipulate Him the way we do other

human beings. We cannot deceive or delude Him. We cannot put pressure on Him to bow to our preferences. We cannot play our little games with One who does not change, who is so consistent He never fails to come through.

Some Twentieth-Century Christians are too flippant with Christ. The modern church and its soulish leaders treat Him as though He were just another human being. Even the music they play and almost meaningless lyrics they sing about Him reflect a lack of proper respect for Heaven's Royalty. Too often He is merely regarded with the same low, crude esteem given to a rock star or Hollywood celebrity.

Whereas the latter all fade away into oblivion, He endures forever. Yet, He is not given the great honour and respect His character deserves, His glory demands.

We deceive ourselves if we believe that somehow our spectacular displays of prophecy, tongues or knowledge can compensate for our lack of credibility. We are totally deluded if we think that special miracles, great gifts or enormous understanding of the Bible can be offered as a substitute to Christ for conduct which is contemptible in failing to honour Him.

Hyperactivity is no substitute for the quiet, strong love of God evident in a life that knows Christ and loves the company of His Spirit.

In fact, in this verse under consideration, God's Spirit makes clear to us that all the prominence of prophecy will one day come to an end. All the spectacular means of communication, language, tongues and their interpretation, will cease. The emphasis and importance we attach to knowledge, understanding and information will simply vanish into oblivion.

Yet, is it not strange that we are constantly being deluded to believe that these are the things to which we should devote our time? We are told by preachers and teachers that these are the supreme attainments of life. We are urged by our religious leaders to believe that the greatest thing in all the world is to be totally immersed in the gripping activities of prophecy, communication or acquisition of knowledge.

Not that these are not good and desirable. They are. The trouble is, they simply do not last. Nor are they the loftiest purposes to which we can give ourselves.

Perhaps the most important single sentence written in this whole book is contained in the next few lines. *A person can give his life to no greater good than Christ Himself. God formed us for Himself. We only find our fulfillment in Him.*

To devote ourselves to anything less or anyone else is to actually deprive both ourselves and Him of His highest purposes for us. It is to settle for less than His grandest aspirations for us. It is to come down to the end of our brief lives, only to discover in dismay that in failing to truly love Him, we have failed altogether.

At the risk of annoying the reader, I simply must repeat here that this is precisely why Our Lord Jesus Christ was so very shattering in His earnest statement made in Matthew 7:21-23. I urge you to read this passage quietly and sincerely, in private, allowing Christ's Spirit to speak to you from it.

No matter how highly we may esteem prophecy and all that it means, including the proclamation of the Gospel, no matter how skilled we may become in mass communication or personal persuasiveness, no matter how remarkable and extensive our accumulated knowledge, either secular or biblical—none of them will last throughout eternity.

All are passing—all are transient—all fade away.

Yet God Our Father goes on in glory.

Christ continues in His magnificent constancy.

His Holy Spirit remains ever the same.

This is the durable, eternal, never-failing life of the everlasting One. It is the love of God being continually imparted to those of us open to receive Him and know Him daily. And this in essence is life eternal—without end (see John 17:3).

11

*"For we know in part, and
we prophesy in part. But when
that which is perfect is come,
then that which is in part shall
be done away. When I was a child,
I spake as a child, I understood
as a child, I thought as a child:
but when I became a man,
I put away childish things."*

(1 Cor. 13:9–11)

THE PERFECTION AND MATURITY OF GOD'S LOVE

These three verses disclose that man's knowledge at best is only partial. The most brilliant human intellect only dimly comprehends the complete scope of what can be known. The most esteemed scholar understands but a fraction of the full knowledge available to God.

Obviously this concept applies to both secular and spiritual verities. It is a universal principle that applies to all men of all time. There is never an end to the new discoveries which are to be made, either in the laws that govern the cosmos or the love of Christ that ultimately consummates God's plans for the created universe.

This remarkable revelation given to us by God's Gracious Spirit is valid not only for the great ongoing purposes of Our Father in the immensity of the universe but also in the intimacy of my own inner spirit as His child. The eventual completion and consummation of His good intentions for the entire cosmos, for both heaven and earth, are just as potent for my own personal perfection and maturity as His child.

In other words, God's great work that is under-way, in the majesty of the whole universe, is likewise in progress within the soul of a single man. It is inevitable that this be the case. All is change. All is in transition. All is moving towards final perfection within the generous purposes of God's grace.

Often we look around us, both at the world scene and the private lives of God's people, and wonder if this can be so. We tend to doubt, sometimes, the sovereignty of Christ in the cosmos. There are occasions when our faith in the sure Word of God's Spirit falters at the sight of sin and sorrow so prevalent in the human experience.

Part of the reason for our dismay and our doubts is our incomplete knowledge of God's great and good intentions. We are ill-informed about His pure and majestic purposes both for the planet and His people upon it. Too often the pastors in our pulpits are not attuned to the stimulating intentions of Our Lord in the divine dimension. All they see is the sickness, the despair of a sin-cursed society.

Dismayed and almost hopeless, many Christians struggle with the sordidness that surrounds them. Grappling with the evil of their world, they are dis-couraged by the constant conflict with the enemy of their souls and the downward pull of sin.

Yet the great good cheer given to us here is that God's love changes all of that. The life of Christ at work within us is re-creating us into mature men and women of God. The relentless Spirit of the Most High is everywhere active in bringing history to its supreme conclusion—whether that history be for the entire cosmos or the story of a single soul saved by God's grace. "For God has allowed us to know the secret of his plan, and it is this: he purposes in his sovereign will that everything that exists in Heaven or earth shall find its perfection and fulfillment in him. And here is the staggering thing—that in all which will one day belong to him we have been promised a share (since we were long ago destined for this by the one who achieves his purposes by his sovereign will), so that we, as the first to put our confidence in Christ, may bring praise to his glory!" (Eph. 1:9-12, Phillips).

This is all great good news. It is good cheer for Christians. It is Christ's view of coming perfection.

God's great love for us, His children, for His own amazingly created universe, for all His unseen ministering spirits is such that it must find its ultimate fulfillment in perfection. He would not be God very God if it were less!

This should give us enormous encouragement. It is an assurance, a hope, an anticipation that stirs us to the depths. It quickens our confidence in Christ, stimulates our trust in Our Father's faithfulness, makes our spirits sing with joy as we "see" with spiritual vision what God's Spirit is achieving.

He is at work in us changing us from glory to glory. He is re-creating us to be conformed to the character of Christ. He is actively leading us to follow in His footsteps.

All of this is part of growing up into the maturity which He has purposed for us, a progressive process. It is a life of moving into the godliness of Our Father.

This is His best intention for us.

This is His great love for us.

This is His life in us.

Many Christians are alarmed and dismayed by the idea of perfection. They need not be. It is an inspiring and wondrous design intended by Our Loving Father for our completion as His people.

It was never His intention that we should remain as mere infants, tiny tots, our nourishment only in milk, barely able to crawl around in a cradle. His profound longing, as with a human parent, is that we should grow up in Him. We should become strong in His Spirit. We should mature into men and women who have His mind, His will, His life, delighting to walk with Him.

Each of us are at different stages of development in our life with Christ. We may be just a newborn babe, or a happy youngster, an adventuresome teenager, a young adult, or a sedate senior. Still each of us can be perfect—complete individuals at our stage in life.

A tiny child in the cradle is a perfect human being for his particular level of life at that point in time. Yet we would never claim he is a mature man. So, likewise, in the spiritual realm, it is essential for us to see that each of us can be "perfect" in Christ as God's child, even though less than mature in understanding and judgment.

But it is never God's will that we remain small, weak and helpless. His desire is always that we will put away childish things; be done with childish behaviour and mature into well-developed characters of strength and courage in Christ. All of this is an integral part of God's love for us and just as surely an essential action of Christ's life in us.

The previous paragraph should not be misunderstood here. It does not imply that we are to reject our childlike attitude of faith and love toward Our Father. It does not mean that we lose our childlike trust in Christ. It does not infer that we forget our childlike readiness to follow the gentle leading of God's Holy Spirit. No indeed!

What is intended for us is to know and understand clearly that Christ calls us to change, to growth, in our conduct, our conversation and in our character. He expects that we will achieve our goals with Him. He longs to see us become strong in the power of His might. He looks for the same signs of spiritual maturity in us as a human parent looks for in his offspring.

There are seven of these. And if in fact a person claims to be born again into the family of God, it is appropriate and proper for us to see these sure changes in his life and behaviour. If they are lacking, we have no option but to doubt the validity of a person's claim to be a child of God.

1. A newborn infant must immediately begin to inhale air from the new atmosphere around him. The doctor who delivers the child may even slap him to compel the newborn to draw in oxygen from the air in order for him to survive.

A born-again child of God immediately becomes aware that he is surrounded with a brand-new atmosphere of spiritual life. Through meditation and communion, the child must begin to draw new life from above, from the very wind of God's Spirit that enfolds it.

2. A healthy, sturdy newborn child soon learns to cry out lustily to his parents. He has strong lungs, not

only to inhale fresh air, but also to give loud voice to all his needs.

Likewise with the newborn child of God. The inner longings, yearnings and needs find prompt expression in prayer, in cries to Christ. There is an immediate communication established between the two. The person who finds it well-nigh impossible, or unnecessary, to pray and beseech God as Father has not been born into His family.

3. The normal, healthy human youngster develops a hearty appetite. Every few hours he must be fed. He seems to have an almost insatiable hunger and thirst for constant nourishment.

The result is he clamors for food. He puts on weight. He increases in height. He begins to grow.

A person born from above by the Spirit of God also has an enormous appetite for spiritual food. There is an insatiable thirst for the Scriptures. God's Word becomes meat and drink. Before long young Christians are not satisfied with just the "mere milk" of early infancy. They crave strong meat for maturity.

Again there is good cause to wonder about the man or woman who claims to be a child of God, yet never takes the time to read God's Word, to fill heart and mind with spiritual truth. The Bible remains a closed book to such a person.

4. As a normal human child matures, he very quickly comes to distinguish his parents from others around him. He senses in a very special way the loving bond of "belonging" to his mother and father.

He revels in the warmth and affection shown by the parents. He smiles and snuggles comfortably into the strong embrace of the arms that cradle and surround him with security and love.

So it should be with the child of God, the one who comes to know and love Him as Father. Here there is no fear, no apprehension, no hesitancy at His nearness.

Those of us who truly enjoy the love of Our Father revel in the closeness of our relationship to Him. All through our day we sense His strong arms around us. We relax in His warm embrace. We sense His smile upon us. We are reassured. We are content. We cherish His affection. We smile back.

All is well!

God is not some remote deity far off in space.

He is my Father! He is here! He is at hand! He is attentive to my every need! I am His! He is mine!

Oh, the wonder of His love!

5. The maturing human youngster soon identifies his siblings. He recognizes brothers or sisters. He learns that a special bond of common heritage binds them all together in a single family.

Likewise for the maturing Christian. We soon see that we are not the only child in the family of God. We have become part of a very large and privileged group. Not only is Christ our Saviour, Our Lord, Our Sovereign, He also deigns to call us His brothers and sisters. He is the eldest brother. We have a special affinity and respect for Him.

Beyond this we feel a special kinship and fellowship with other children of God whom we learn to love deeply.

6. The healthy, growing young person in a human family wishes to get past crawling on the floor. He wants to walk. He learns to run. He even becomes strong enough to leap, jump, climb mountains, and keep company with his strong father.

So for the growing child of God. It becomes a special joy to walk with God Our Father. There is enormous excitement in keeping company with Christ. There is a wondrous adventure in being led to new heights by the loving guidance of God's Gracious Spirit.

7. In this constant exposure to a human parent, the young person actually takes on the traits and characteristics of the parent. We become like those we live with.

It is precisely the same in our life with Christ! We actually *become like Him*. We take on His very character. We are matured by exposure to His company. We are conformed and perfected in His companionship. It is all a part of the perfect union of His life and love. What a wonder!

"('The Lord' means the Spirit, and wherever the Spirit of the Lord is, there is open freedom.) But we all mirror the glory of the Lord with face unveiled, and so we are being transformed into the same likeness as himself, passing from one glory to another—for this comes of the Lord the Spirit" (2 Cor. 3:17-18, Moffatt).

*"For now we see
through a glass,
darkly; but then
face to face:
now I know in
part; but then
shall I know
even as also
I am known."*

(1 Cor. 13:12)

KNOWING AND UNDERSTANDING THE LOVE OF GOD

Again and again the point has been made in this book that our comprehension, either secular or spiritual, is at best limited. Most emphatically is that so when it comes to a clear understanding of the true character of Christ.

His life, His love, His awesome attributes of integrity, strength, compassion, mercy, justice and righteousness outshine our human condition like the midday sun excels the darkness of night. His glory and His grandeur are of such magnificence that we dare not gaze upon them in their full-orbed splendor without being blinded by their intensity.

Our human eyes, our human understanding, our human spiritual awareness is veiled by our hardness of heart, and dullness of spirit, our stained souls. And the nearer we draw to Him, the more acute becomes our awareness of our own undone condition.

The closer any child of God comes to Christ, the more he realizes how desperately he needs to be purified, cleansed and searched to stand before The

Most High. The utter intensity of His impeccable person bows our haughty hearts, crumbles our proud spirits, sending us to our knees in humility to cry out as Isaiah did, "Woe is me! for I am undone; because I am a man of unclean lips, and I dwell in the midst of a people of unclean lips; for mine eyes have seen the King, the Lord of hosts" (Isa. 6:5).

It is this acute awareness of the matchless purity of Christ's person which is a hallmark of the man or woman who walks in close communion with Him. There is an aura of awe, respect, reverence and great regard for God. He is spoken to with enormous deference. He is treated with the utmost honour. He is held in the highest esteem.

This does not preclude loving Him dearly. It does not mean His companionship cannot be cherished. But it does imply that He is supreme and I am at best a mere man upon whom His bountiful grace has been bestowed in making me His child.

Because of all this, it is only dimly that I can perceive the supreme perfection of Christ's character. At times I can catch fleeting glimpses of His true glory reflected as it were from the mirrored events of life that He has arranged around me.

Here and there startling shafts of light glance off the walls of my world to illuminate the darkness with His splendor. Yet, even then, the light is only dimly perceived because in the very nature of things whatever we see comes to us in reverse, left to right, and right to left, as in a mirror. Always, ever, our human limitations require that an adjustment be made and compensation allowed for our fallibility.

As long as our spirits are confined and restricted

by our human condition, our true comprehension of the greatness of God's love will be only a dim perception of Christ's perfection, blurred by our partial blindness, dulled by our doubting souls, distorted by our finite understanding and feeble faith.

Yet, in spite of all this inner struggle "to see Him" as He truly is, there burns bright the hope and assurance that one day we shall see Him face to face. It will be as if the opaque veil of our humanity is torn away. The encroaching cataracts of our spiritual blindness will be removed. Then we shall see Him without restriction in all His beauty.

Then, our spirits set free in wondrous adoration, we shall sense that incredible change that will conform us to His own character. Bless His name forever!

"As for me, I will behold thy face in righteousness: I shall be satisfied, when I awake, with thy likeness" (Ps. 17:15).

Then imperfection will have put on perfection. Oh, what glorious emancipation awaits the child of God! What stirring hope God gives His people! What a complete and sublime consummation for the Christian!

In the meantime, however, it is appropriate and proper that we should clearly understand the methods and means God uses to reveal Himself to us. While we are still here in the earth scene, it is essential for us to grasp precisely how we can "see God," even though it be dimly at best.

He has arranged four sets of mirrors around us from which there is reflected to us, like light from the walls, the very character of His own life and love.

On the one side there is the actual expression of

His person in the life of Christ, Jesus of Nazareth. "Christ is the visible expression of the invisible God" (Col. 1:15, Phillips).

In His conduct, His conversation and His character, we see without tarnish or inconsistency the love of God. From His life we get startling insights into the depths of divine nature.

As we meditate quietly over His short sojourn as a man amongst us, yet God very God, an enormous impact is made upon our spirits by His person.

Expose your poor soul to His life and He will change you so that you are never quite the same again.

The second great mirrored wall which God has put in place for us is His wondrous Word. It is the divine disclosure of His own self. It is a shining revealer of His true character.

As we look into it there glances from it bright beams of One who is totally trustworthy, utterly reliable, forever faithful. He is no mere man. We see instead, even if only feebly, the stirring grandeur of Our God, Our Father, Our Monarch arrayed in majesty, power and might.

Yet with all of that, we "see" Him who loves us with an unexplainable, unshakable, eternal love that draws us to Him.

The third wall of mirrors arranged around us to reveal something of the character of God is the natural universe. The beauty of trees, fields, streams, hills, forests and oceans reflect the pure loveliness of Our Lord.

In ten thousand life forms and uncounted myriads of spheres in space we "see" a dim reflection of the magnificent mind of Christ. In the expanses of ocean, the majesty of mountains and the exquisite artistry of flowers, we catch a hint of the beautiful heart of our caring Father. "For the invisible things of him from the creation of the world are clearly seen, being understood by the things that are made, even his eternal power and Godhead; so that they are without excuse" (Rom. 1:20).

If we are people contrite in spirit, humble in heart, free from human arrogance and its corruption of intellectual pride, we will pause before the wonders of nature and give hearty thanks for Christ's creative artistry.

The fourth wall of reflecting surfaces is made up of all those precious people in whom God resides by His Spirit. From their conduct and gracious words there flashes something of the very life of Christ who indwells them.

In a hundred kind deeds, in a score of selfless, generous gestures, in comforting actions, words of good cheer and hearty encouragement, we see something of the selfless character of Christ. Amid the selfishness and skepticism of human society there sparkles here and there a soul that shines to us a likeness of the love of God.

If men are to see God, even dimly, in this dark and dreary world, they can catch a fleeting glimpse from the wholesome lives of godly men and women in whom He is at work (see Phil. 2:13).

In all of this we can know, only in part, a small fraction of the full-orbed greatness of Our Lord. Yet it is enough to strengthen our spirits and set our souls to singing. We are assured on every side that Christ has come to us. He is here with us. He will not forsake us. All is well!

With this awareness there grows upon us a new
dimension of confidence in Christ. It is the intense
realization that not only is He here, but also that He
fully *knows me*. Or, put in the plainest possible terms,
He completely understands me.

It may well be that I shall never, ever, fully know
or understand all of God's love and concern for me.
I may never comprehend all the impeccable qualities
of His character. But praise to Him for His great
generosity, He fully knows me in every detail and
deals with me in utter integrity.

For the child of God, *to be known by Him* should
be the greatest encouragement in all the world. All
of our lives we are interacting with people who do
not really know us, much less understand us. Many
of our problems in life arise from lack of knowledge
and adequate understanding of one another.

People wear masks to conceal their true character.
They live behind false fronts of propriety. They pretend
to be one thing while living another. A veneer of culture
covers crudeness, cruelty and deception.

It is frightening for most people to realize that
"God knows you through and through!" They feel
threatened by such knowledge.

But for the Christian this is great good news. And
for these three special reasons:

1. God in Christ knows all the intricacies of my
genetic makeup. He is fully aware of all the interre-
lated characteristics which were inherited from my
parents, grandparents and former forebears. He knows
precisely why I am the unique, special person I am.

No one else, not even my parents, knows this much.

In fact I am often an absolute enigma to them.

But God knows me in this intimacy. He under-stands exactly why my inherited features influence me to behave as I do. Consequently only He can treat me with utter integrity and complete understanding, tempered with compassion.

2. Only God in Christ, by His spirit, is fully aware of all the environmental influences which have been brought to bear upon my life since the day of concep-tion.

No human being does, not even my own mother.

It is this infinite, incredible *knowing* that enables Christ to deal with me in dignity, forgiveness and love. He knows all the strains, stresses and pressures that shaped me.

He alone can properly appraise the impact made on me by my parents, my home, my siblings, my schools, my playmates, my teachers, my friends and all other human associates. He knows the experiences, the griefs, the triumphs, the adventures, the work, the impact of books and films and a thousand other influ-ences that molded me as a man.

No one else does or can.

Not even I can fully know myself or understand my behaviour. Is it any wonder, then, He cried from the cross, *"Father, forgive them; for they know not what they do"?* (Luke 23:34).

3. Only God in Christ can clearly comprehend all my thoughts, all my hopes, all my fears, all my imagi-nations, all my emotions, all my deliberate choices, all my subconscious impulses.

And because He does, He deals with me in mercy, kindness, patience, long-suffering, justice and total integrity. Oh, the grandeur and graciousness of such a Saviour, such a Friend, such a *Father*!

It is this dimension of being known to the utmost depth of my being that has drawn me to Christ with unbreakable cords of love—*His love*.

For though He knows the best, He also knows the worst, knows the noble, knows the wrong, and He knows the deep yearnings of my spirit to be like Him. He treats me with utter truth and total understanding.

I dare not try to run a bluff on Him. Yet I can cast myself in fearless contrition upon His compassion. I dare not indulge in hypocritical duplicity. But I can come to Him, anytime, completely assured He fully understands me through and through.

Oh, the marvel of His love! Oh, the wonder of His care! Oh, the greatness of His grace! Hallelujah!

He is mine and I am His forever!

13

*"In this life
we have three
great lasting
qualities—faith,
hope and love."*

(1 Cor. 13:13, Phillips)

THE ENDURING ASPECTS OF FAITH, HOPE AND LOVE

It has been emphasized repeatedly that everything in this life is transient—except God Himself. Only that which is grounded in God endures. All else is subject to change and disintegration.

For this reason, if for no other, man's life, unless founded upon the unchanging character of Christ, comes to nothing. It is a vain show. Like the morning mist, it vanishes into vapour. What remains is but an empty vacuum of no value.

Upon what, then, are we to build our eternal destiny? From what fabric will a man or a woman fashion his/her future? What qualities of life can one count on to outlast our little lives and see us safely into the eternal dimension?

Without hesitation, The Spirit of The Living God assures us that there are three beautiful building materials from which a Christian can construct an indestructible character. They are *faith, hope,* and *love.* All three have one common aspect to them—they last, endure, remain and abide until the dawn of eternity.

The reason they do so is simple to see.

They are essentially grounded in God.

They are basically centered in Christ.

They are ultimately established in His Spirit.

These are the eternal verities which endure.

If a man invests his short life in anything else, his days are spent for naught—wasted, gone with the wind.

Faith, hope and love are not competing qualities in life. They do not stand separately, detached and apart from one another. Quite the opposite! They are a tightly intertwined, three-strand cord, braided together to form the unbreakable line of Christ's character extended to us as our own lifeline of eternal duration.

Our faith in God, if it is to have any dynamic reality at all, is inextricably intertwined with the love of God. The basic reason is so obvious it scarcely needs mentioning here. But we can have confidence only in a totally trustworthy character. We can invest our reliance only in an utterly reliable person if we hope for lasting endurance. We can have quiet faith only in the love of The Eternal Christ if we expect to have it validated in an eternal dimension.

It is the character of Christ which validates our faith in Him. It is the essential integrity of His love which gives vitality to our trust. It is the sterling caliber of His commitments to us which assures us of His constant care.

Our Father's love, justice, truth and mercy are the basic bedrock upon which we build. All our hope, love and strong confidence as Christ's followers are fashioned from the unbreakable fabric of His own impeccable character. It is the raw material of the very life of Christ, the love of God Himself, which is dispensed to us by The Holy Spirit of The Most High in re-creating us.

In all of this, faith is a formidable force which He, The Gracious Spirit of God, imparts to us. It is a generous gift which bestows upon us the capacity to respond to the grace of God. It is, unfortunately, exercised by very few.

Faith is my personal, private, positive response to the character of Christ and to the Word of God, to the extent I will act upon His wishes.

This implies, of course, that I clearly comprehend the integrity of His character. This book has been an earnest endeavour to inform the reader of God's love and character as expressed in the very life of Christ.

It implies, too, that I clearly understand what My Father's will, His wishes, are for me as His child. Such information comes increasingly as one studies, examines and meditates over God's Word. Or to put it in the rather poetic language of the New Testament: *"Faith cometh by hearing, and hearing by the Word of God"* (Rom. 10:17).

The "hearing" spoken of here implies much more than merely receiving audio impulses upon the membranes of the ear. It means a powerful, positive response of my spirit to God's Spirit when He speaks to me.

There are three profound aspects to this process of "hearing" that lead to viable faith in any Christian's life.

1. *I recognize it is God speaking to me.*

The message communicated to me is not merely man's ideas. I am aware that Christ is communing with me. The words He speaks convey to me both *Spirit* and *Life* (see John 6:63).

2. *I respond to His disclosures in a positive action of my will.*

Keen attention is paid to what He says. A willingness to comply with His commands marks my behaviour. I set my will to do His will no matter the personal cost or inconvenience.

3. *I run instantly to do His bidding—always.*

"Hearing" in this way not only builds enormous faith in the daily life of the believer, but also, even more importantly, brings inexpressible pleasure to Christ. For without this faith of active obedience it is impossible to please God. And surely, surely, *surely* if we claim to love Him, the very least we can do to demonstrate our devotion to Him is comply with His wishes.

Our Lord made this entire concept clear to His disciples in His last great discourse with them just before His death. It is iterated and reiterated in John 14–17. This is a passage which every seeking soul who longs to understand the love of God should read and re-read.

There we discover something of the remarkable love of Christ which enables us to invest our faith in Him without fear or hesitation. Such faith, no matter how feeble, will never fail simply because it is grounded in the impeccable character of Christ. It will abide because He abides forever the same. It is constant because His love is constant. It is filled with hope because He is our hope.

It is not the caliber or quantity of our faith that matters. Rather, it is the content of His loving character that counts.

This is why Jesus said that even if we only had as

much faith as a grain of mustard seed, it would be possible to move mountains. Few can truly understand this kind of faith.

I sometimes use the illustration of a young lady falling in love with a handsome young man. She invests enormous faith in him. She builds her hopes of a happy marriage around him. She dreams her dreams of a fine family on the basis of his behaviour during their courtship. She is sure all will be bright and beautiful.

But after the wedding bells have rung and the honeymoon is over, she discovers that her handsome "Prince Charming" is really a rotten rogue. He is unfaithful to her. His character is corrupt. He is full of falsehood and duplicity.

All her dreams crash into rubble.

All her hopes are blown to the winds.

All her longings are swept into oblivion.

Her heart is broken! Her home is a shambles! Her happiness is gone!

Why?

Because she lacked faith in the fellow? No.

Because she was not sincere? No.

Because she did not love him enough? No.

Simply because his character was no good, was false.

She had invested all her confidence in the wrong person. She had put her trust in the wrong place. She had built her hope and love on the wrong kind of character.

Eventually her husband dies. The years go by. She is sure she can never have faith in men again. She is uneasy about them all.

One day a second stranger comes into her life. He seems a much more simple man. He is not pretentious, proud or vain. His sincerity and earnestness attract her.

A tiny spark of faith is ignited within her. Almost in fear and trepidation, she finally decides to try once more. She trusts this one. With no more faith than a grain of mustard seed, she agrees to share life with him.

It turns out he is a person of commendable character. He is honest. He is trustworthy. He is loving and kind.

Her heart is healed. Her home is a bit of heaven. Her fondest hopes come to life. Her happiness is complete.

What made the difference?

Was it the amount of faith she had? No!

Was it her sincerity? No.

It was the superb character of the second man that validated her tiny particle of faith in him. It was his character that guaranteed and totally insured her future contentment.

It is exactly the same with Christ!

He is our bridegroom. We are His people, His church, His followers, His Bride.

Our love, our hope and our faith are and should be grounded only in Him. It is His impeccable character, His perfect conduct, and His utterly trustworthy commitments to us in His Word which honour our hope, validate our faith and confirm our love for Him.

It is for this reason and only for this reason that our faith, hope, and love for Him endure. They abide because He abides faithful. They endure because He endures ever trustworthy. They remain ever sure only because He remains steadfast, the same forever.

Once we see this tremendous truth we will no longer fasten our attention on our own feeble faith. Instead we will lift our gaze upon the glory of Him who is totally trustworthy. Our hope instead of being set upon those things which can be seen will be centered in the consummate character of Christ who will never fail us. Our love, rather than being lavished upon the transient things of time, will be poured out in overflowing gratitude to Our Father who loves us with His everlasting love.

At last our lives will have found their sure, strong, peaceful resting place in the companionship of Christ.

As I have said before and must repeat here, *"The great glory of Our God is His character, and His character is His glory!"*

We simply *must* grasp this truth if we are ever to become the triumphant people of God who will make an indelible imprint on our generation. Our faith, our hope, our love—yes, indeed our very life—has force, power and impact in direct proportion to the extent we clearly comprehend the character of Christ.

He and He alone is the object of our faith. He is the bedrock of our hope. He is the epicenter of our own love. We are in Him. He is in us. Therein lies our endurance amid all the changing scenes and circumstances of this unpredictable life scene.

Down to the very last day that we tread the tangled trails of our earthly sojourn we will find that *"faithful is he that calleth you, who also will do it"* (1 Thess. 5:24).

Then when the call comes to us "to come home," even through the door of death and beyond the grave, our sure and serene confidence will be in Him. For then, and only then, will our faith be turned to spiritual sight, for we shall see Him face to face. And then our hope shall be turned to the living reality of heaven and home for we shall be in His visible presence forever and ever (see 1 Thess. 4).

Such stirring and thrilling expectations set before us as His people are but a part of His gracious, generous love for us. Not only for all of this life does He supply us with faith, hope and love, but also far beyond. Into the endless avenues of eternity His love never fails us.

Praise His wonderful name!

14

"But the greatest of these is charity [love]. Follow after charity [love]."

(1 Cor. 13:13–14:1)

FOLLOW CHRIST—
HE IS LOVE
HE IS GREATEST

The final, quiet conclusion to which God's Spirit leads us in this discussion on God's remarkable love is simply this: *love is the greatest of all.* There is no fanfare about it. There is no bugling of trumpets or blaring of brass.

It is one of those calm, categorical statements of truth that are so typical of Christ. Either we accept this as fact or we reject it as folly. Most people prefer to believe that money, wealth, success, pleasure, adventure or fame are the greatest.

Within the church itself, people may not be quite so crass. Still multitudes prefer to devote most of their time and attention to more spectacular and sensational activities than living quietly in sincere love.

It is fascinating to have huge building projects under way. It is exciting to hold large conventions with thousands in attendance. It is fantastic to have loud music with a powerful beat that attracts crowds of young people. It is great to see faith healers performing miracles. It is magnificent to watch gifted speakers storm up and down the platform shouting into microphones and television cameras. It is terrific to tell of the millions of miles traveled on tours to the most remote ends of the earth.

Amid all of this self-centered behaviour the still, small voice of God's Spirit reminds us—*love is the greatest.*

Why? Why is this so?

Simply because *God is love.*

We do not have His love unless we have Him.

It is a most grievous mistake, often perpetuated by preachers and teachers, to think God dispenses His love to His people apart from Himself. Many labour under the false delusion that Our Father sits aloof, far off in His Heaven, dropping down little gift-wrapped packages of love to those who request it.

Not so!

We only have the love of God in our lives to the extent we have God in our lives. We only have the character of Christ reflected in our conduct to the extent we have Christ resident within us. We only have the fruit of God's Gracious Spirit born within our attitudes and actions to the extent God's Spirit actually indwells our minds, emotions and wills.

This is the basic, inescapable concept that eludes so many Christians. Yet it is the secret to experiencing God's love.

To know God in Christ is the greatest thing in all the universe.

There is no greater good in all the world.

There is no greater end to which we can give ourselves than to abide in Christ and allow Him to abide in us.

There is no greater life than that of laying down ourselves in love and gratitude as He laid down His life for us.

"For God so loved the world, that he gave his only begotten Son, that whosoever believeth in him should not perish, but have everlasting life" (John 3:16).

"Hereby perceive we the love of God, because he laid down his life for us: and we ought to lay down our lives for the brethren" (1 John 3:16).

He made us for Himself in love. He chose us in love to be His children. He longs over us in love to be conformed to His character. He delights in us in love as His sons and daughters who walk with Him.

From the world's viewpoint there is nothing remarkable or earth-shaking about this. It is to be despised.

Nor is the world alone in its wrong evaluation of what is man's ultimate end and aim. Within the community of Christendom, there are many discordant voices and false teachers who would divert God's people to other purposes.

From their pulpits, their media broadcasts, their magazines, books and pamphlets, a host of leaders insist on other priorities. They scream loudly or suggest very subtly that the greatest issues in life are:

Peace! Peace! Peace! at any price.

Political reform.

Social concern.

The exercise of faith in many forms.

Mass evangelism.

Feeding of famine-ridden people.

Mighty miracles.

The gifts of the Spirit.

It was no different in A.D. 55-60.

The church at Corinth was totally absorbed in sensuality. It was a body of believers preoccupied with the sensational. It was caught up in following every new fad that was spawned by false teachers in the spiritual realm.

So, amid God's clear and explicit instructions as to the role of His gifts to the church, the startling and sobering command is given: *"Follow love! Follow me!"*

It is as if in the midst of all the flighty ecstasies of the moment, a direct appeal is made to all men to come back to the ultimate reality; to come back to the consummate concern of God Himself; to come back to love—to Christ, who gives Himself that we might live.

"Follow Christ!" is God's divine command.

This brings us up sharply. It slices cleanly through the melee of conflicting concerns within the church. It calls us back to the supreme good in life. We do not have to debate the issues any longer. We need not be in the dark about our highest aim or greatest good.

It is to follow Christ.

Because I have dealt with this subject in such depth in the book *A Shepherd Looks at Psalm 23* (pages 75–80), there is no need to go over that ground here again. In that volume the matter of "following Christ" is approached from the very practical aspect of our personal, daily life with Christ, what it means in actual cost to *follow love* in an unloving world.

Here at the conclusion of this study, my desire is to reveal to the reader a little of what it means *to follow love* from God's viewpoint.

First and foremost, let it be said emphatically that

to follow Christ, as He so often invited men to do when He was here amongst us, is not to be bound into following rigid rules and regulations. It is not to be inhibited and constricted by certain inexorable instructions that must be followed religiously.

No! Ten thousand times no!

To be called by Christ, to follow Him into His love, is to be invited to enter the freedom of marvelous sonship with God Our Father. It means coming to enjoy the remarkable friendship of Christ our dearest One. It leads us into the exciting liberty of enjoying the constant comradeship of His Holy Spirit, our counselor, who will lead us aright.

This is what it is to follow Christ ... to love God.

In all of this sublime interaction between God and me, the enfolding love of Christ that surrounds my life and pervades my spirit leads me to loyalty, unity of purpose and overwhelming gratitude. *I love because He first loved me.*

Christ's desires become my desires.

His standards become my standards.

His work becomes my work in the world.

His will becomes my will—always!

This is not to be bound into grudging servitude. Just the opposite! It is to be set free to follow The Most High as a comrade on the high road of a noble, splendid life.

The consequences of such intimate companionship with Christ are enormous. No longer am I a mere man drifting in despair through the uncharted depths of life's stormy experiences. No longer am I tossed to and fro like flotsam by the adverse waves of my years here. No longer am I dismayed by the powerful tides of time that seem to run deep against me.

Why? Because He who is in me and with me is greater, far greater, than any elemental force at work in the world. It is the powerful life of Christ within who counteracts the down-drag of sin. It is the expulsive energy and force of His presence that puts to rout the enemy of my soul. It is the purifying influence of His character that counteracts the corrosion of my old self nature.

His love, His life, His light dispel the darkness, flooding my life with goodwill, hope, faith and love.

So in His calm assurance I find repose—*all is well!*

Beyond all of this there comes the acute awareness that because of this relationship with God, all things do actually work out for my eventual benefit and well-being. It matters not how painful the paroxysms of life may be or how crushing its circumstances, Christ is arranging them for my ultimate good.

Such strength and such confidence can come only to the person who has responded decisively to The Master's call, who has chosen deliberately to follow Him no matter how acute the cost, who has come to love The Lord with intense loyalty.

The Spirit of God puts it this way, "We know that all things work together for good to them that love God, to them who are the called according to his purpose" (Rom. 8:28).

This is not a matter of mere wishful thinking. It is more than just hoping it might happen. It is the profoundly moving reality of a life bound up in the strong purposes of my Father for me as His child. At every turn in the long trail of my years I can look back to see that His hand has been upon me for good. His presence has gone with me to protect from harm and to preserve in patience. Everywhere I see living, irrefutable evidence of His love, care and compassion that surround my steps. My ways have been ordered and arranged by His Gracious Spirit in incredible love.

It is difficult to describe in language the inner serenity, the exquisite contentment from enjoying the companionship of Christ in this way. There is such a deep, satisfying dimension of delight to it that the most winsome attractions of the world pale beside it. They seem so fickle, so feeble, so fleeting. They fade to nothing.

He becomes the enduring, wondrous One.

Finally, it is appropriate to point out that the man or woman who earnestly "follows love" by keeping company with Christ is the one whose prayers will be answered. Not only will their own personal walk with God be the supreme pleasure of life, but also the impact of that love relationship will reach to the ends of the earth. Enormous blessing and benefit will emanate from their communion with Christ to touch uncounted multitudes. The Spirit of The Most High who resides in such a life will move in and through it to touch ten thousand other hearts.

The reason for this is not always understood. It is because the soul in harmony with Christ, in unity with His Spirit, sensitive to His Father's wishes, will pray in accordance with His will. Such petitions and intercessions are bound to be honoured simply because they originate and consummate with God!

Out of this harmonious and loving interaction

between God and man, more great things are achieved upon the planet than this weary world has ever dreamed of. For the Christian who daily delights in the love of God, who literally revels in the company of Christ, prayer and praise and upwelling gratitude come as naturally as breathing air, drinking water or eating fruit. For in actual fact the very love of God, the life of Christ, the presence of His Spirit become the ever-present environment that energizes his total being. It is "in Him we live, and move, and have our being" (Acts 17:28).

Nor is this some exclusive experience reserved only for an elite group. It can be the joyous, personal testimony and quiet strength of anyone called of Christ. The choice is ours how we shall respond to His gracious, generous overtures of love. For those who do decide irrevocably to share life with Him there comes the remarkable assurance: *"I have become absolutely convinced that neither death nor life, neither messenger of Heaven nor monarch of earth, neither what happens today nor what may happen tomorrow, neither a power from on high nor a power from below, nor anything else in God's whole world has any power to separate us from the love of God in Jesus Christ our Lord!"* (Rom. 8:38-39, Phillips).

Amen and Amen!

CHRISTIAN HERALD ASSOCIATION AND ITS MINISTRIES

CHRISTIAN HERALD ASSOCIATION, founded in 1878, publishes The Christian Herald Magazine, one of the leading interdenominational religious monthlies in America. Through its wide circulation, it brings inspiring articles and the latest news of religious developments to many families. From the magazine's pages came the initiative for CHRISTIAN HERALD CHILDREN and THE BOWERY MISSION, two individually supported not-for-profit corporations.

CHRISTIAN HERALD CHILDREN, established in 1894, is the name for a unique and dynamic ministry to disadvantaged children, offering hope and opportunities which would not otherwise be available for reasons of poverty and neglect. The goal is to develop each child's potential and to demonstrate Christian compassion and understanding to children in need.

Mont Lawn is a permanent camp located in Bushkill, Pennsylvania. It is the focal point of a ministry which provides a healthful "vacation with a purpose" to children who without it would be confined to the streets of the city. Up to 1000 children between the age of 7 and 11 come to Mont Lawn each year.

Christian Herald Children maintains year-round contact with children by means of a *City Youth Ministry.* Central to its philosophy is the belief that only through sustained relationships and demonstrated concern can individual lives be truly enriched. Special emphasis is on individual guidance, spiritual and family counseling and tutoring. This follow-up ministry to inner-city children culminates for many in financial assistance toward higher education and career counseling.

THE BOWERY MISSION, located at 227 Bowery, New York City, has since 1879 been reaching out to the lost men on the Bowery, offering them what could be their last chance to rebuild their lives. Every man is fed, clothed and ministered to. Countless numbers have entered the 90-day residential rehabilitation program at the Bowery Mission. A concentrated ministry of counseling, medical care, nutrition therapy, Bible study and Gospel services awakens a man to spiritual renewal within himself.

These ministries are supported solely by the voluntary contributions of individuals and by legacies and bequests. Contributions are tax deductible. Checks should be made out either to CHRISTIAN HERALD CHILDREN or to THE BOWERY MISSION.

Administrative Office: 40 Overlook Drive, Chappaqua, New York 10514
Telephone: (914) 769-9000